Scientists Anonymous

Great Stories of Women in Science

Patricia Fara

Published in the UK in 2005
by Icon Books Ltd., The Old Dairy,
Brook Road, Thriplow, Cambridge SG8 7RG
email: wizard@iconbooks.co.uk
www.iconbooks.co.uk/wizard

Sold in the UK by Faber and Faber Ltd.,
3 Queen Square, London WC1N 3AU
or their agents

Distributed in the UK by TBS Ltd., Frating
Distribution Centre, Colchester Road,
Frating Green, Colchester CO7 7DW

Published in Australia in 2005
by Allen & Unwin Pty. Ltd., PO Box 8500,
83 Alexander Street, Crows Nest, NSW 2065

Distributed in Canada by Penguin Books Canada,
90 Eglinton Avenue East, Suite 700, Toronto,
Ontario M4P 2YE

ISBN 1 84046 574 3

Typesetting by Wayzgoose

Printed and bound in Great Britain by
William Clowes Ltd, Beccles, Suffolk

DEDICATION

For Clarissa and the future

Acknowledgements

Many scholars and campaigners – predominantly, but not exclusively, women – have helped to change attitudes towards women in science. I am indebted to them, both for what they have achieved and for what I have learnt from them. Many of their insights have found their way into *Scientists Anonymous*, but I have drawn especially heavily from three sources: the *Biographical Dictionary of Women in Science* edited by Marilyn Ogilvie and Joy Harvey (Routledge, 2000); Londa Schiebinger's *The Mind has no Sex? Women in the Origins of Modern Science* (Harvard University Press, 1989); and the essays in *Natural Eloquence: Women Reinscribe Science* (University of Wisconsin Press, 1989), edited by Barbara Gates and Ann Shteir. I am also extremely grateful to Simon Flynn at Wizard for his enthusiasm and invaluable suggestions.

Contents

Prologue

Men have had every advantage of us in telling their own story. Education has been theirs in so much higher a degree; the pen has been in their hands.

Jane Austen, *Persuasion*, 1818

HAVE YOU EVER looked through a book and wondered who wrote all those poems and witty sayings by Anon? The authors' families, friends and publishers must have known who they were. So why were their identities concealed and their names forgotten?

Virginia Woolf, the famous Bloomsbury set writer, believed she had the answer. 'I would venture to guess', she wrote, 'that Anon, who wrote so many books without signing them, was a woman'. In the past, women often used to publish anonymously to avoid drawing attention to themselves – a most undignified way for women to behave. For centuries, women were meant to occupy themselves by looking after their home, their husband and their children; any time left over should be spent embroidering, reading or playing music. If they needed to earn their living, then they could become a governess or the companion of a rich, elderly lady.

Woolf felt very bitter about women's poor education

and their lack of freedom. Her life changed dramatically in 1904, when her dominating father died and she started a new and exciting life in London. Woolf started campaigning for women to have the same opportunities as men to write and think, to travel and vote, to study and party.

That very same year, 1904, another woman made a major breakthrough towards obtaining equality for women in science. She was called **Hertha Ayrton**, and she achieved a female first by reading out her own paper at London's Royal Society. Before then, although the Royal Society had occasionally published articles about original research by women, they had never been allowed to present their own work. Instead, they remained hidden behind a male relative or friend who read their lecture for them.

Like Woolf, Ayrton fought vigorously for female equality. Also like Woolf, Ayrton was liberated by the death of the powerful man in her life: after her husband died, she became far more militant and joined the suffragette movement. Ayrton often denounced sexual discrimination in science, and she told a journalist: 'I do not agree with sex being brought into science at all. The idea of "woman and science" is completely irrelevant. Either a woman is a good scientist, or she is not; in any case she should be given opportunities, and her work should be studied from the scientific, not the sex, point of view.' Unfortunately, these words still need repeating today.

Just like the anonymous authors whose identities

have vanished from poetry books, countless unacknow-ledged women have participated in science over the centuries. They have carried out experiments, built up collections, recorded observations, discussed theories, translated foreign books, illustrated apparatus and classi-fied specimens. These women struggled against oppres-sion and fought to practise science, but now they are scarcely remembered. Many of their names have van-ished for ever, but some of them can be retrieved.

By rescuing these women from obscurity and telling their stories, *Scientists Anonymous* shows how important women have been in science's history. Despite their lack of opportunities, women did make vital contribu-tions to the growth of science. Male scientists are cele-brated because their names appear on title pages, but their anonymous colleagues also deserve to be com-memorated.

PRESENT

Present

She was the kind of wife who looks out of her front door in the morning and, if it's raining, apologizes.
Fay Weldon, *Heart of the Country,* 1987

POLITICIANS CLAIM THAT all children have equal opportunities, but among professional scientists there are still far fewer women than men. One easy explanation is to say that brains are linked to sex – that girls and boys are born with different types of innate ability. This is a very old belief. Traditional nursery rhymes reinforce the idea that boys are expected to be nasty ...

> *Frogs and snails*
> *And puppy-dogs' tails*
> *That's what little boys are made of.*

... whereas girls should be all sweetness and light ...

> *Sugar and spice*
> *And all things nice*
> *That's what little girls are made of.*

Such biased sentiments may be old, but they are still deeply ingrained. Many people argue that it is a waste of time teaching girls physics, because they are inherently incapable of grappling with mathematical equations and lack a good 3-D imagination. But although it may (or may not) be true that boys and girls start out in life with dissimilar brains, there are other possibilities to explore.

One approach is to think about how children are brought up. Baby girls and boys are treated differently right from the minute they are born, and that encourages them to develop in contrasting ways. Another way of thinking about today's problems is to realise how slowly old attitudes die out. The rate of change is accelerating, but it takes many many generations for prejudices to disappear completely.

Women nowadays have far more opportunities than even 30 years ago. That may seem a long time, but it's extremely short compared with centuries of tradition. There are still people alive who remember the First World War, so it makes sense that discrimination taking place then should have survived up to now. The German mathematician Emmy Noether, who lived in the early 20th century, was so brilliant that Albert Einstein called her 'a creative mathematical genius', but when she applied to become a lecturer, she was turned down. The university authorities gave what now seems a very strange reason: 'What will our soldiers think when they return to the University and find that they are expected to learn at the feet of a woman?'

Girls are now encouraged to take science at school, and are given the same education as boys. As the barriers of sex discrimination tumble, girls are outstripping boys in national examinations. Their success might infuriate some men, but should not really be surprising. On average, girls do better than boys in intelligence (IQ) tests, which are designed to pick out innate ability independently of how good a school is or how hard someone works. When IQ tests were first introduced in schools, the examiners discovered to their dismay that girls consistently got higher scores. Because they wanted to conceal this embarrassing discrepancy, they adjusted the marking scheme so that boys and girls seemed to be performing equally.

Massaging the results of IQ tests was just one of the many obstacles erected to prevent women from becoming high scientific achievers. Even now, there are many subtle ways in which girls are led to believe – often subconsciously – that they are not as clever or as worthwhile as their brothers. Psychological restrictions can be extremely effective for preventing women from behaving independently. When people are trapped in unpleasant, subordinated situations, it is difficult for them to escape because they have been conditioned into believing that they are inferior.

Countries like Britain and the USA pride themselves on providing equal opportunities, but in practice they have far more men than women in science's best-paid jobs. Although roughly the same numbers of boys and girls enter university to study science and maths, the higher up the career ladder you look, the fewer women there are.

Women seem to get stuck in their careers as if there were an invisible barrier, a glass ceiling, preventing them from climbing any higher. The disparity between the sexes increases as people progress through their careers. Even though around half of science students are female, within a few years there are more men than women in scientific jobs. While the men get promoted, women either leave science or stay at lower levels. Fewer women than men go on to do research, and even fewer of those become lecturers or laboratory directors. And at the professorship and senior management levels, only a very small fraction are women.

Two basic facts about women in top-level science are clear: there are far fewer female than male scientists, and far more women do biological sciences than mathematical ones. In Britain, every year around 4,000 students in science or engineering get a doctorate, that essential qualification for becoming a professional scientist – but there are two men for every woman. Although there are far fewer women in total, *more* women than men get doctorates in biological subjects. For maths and computer science, the ratio is the other way round – there are over five men for every woman.

The details for each country are different, but the general pattern is the same all over the world. These statistics suggest all sorts of questions. Are men really better at maths and physics than women? Why do women outnumber men in the life sciences? Are men and women born with different sorts of brains? Or do they start out equal and get steered apart as they grow up? Do women choose not to apply for high positions, or are they unfairly discriminated against?

I believe that history can help to answer some of these questions. In order to understand the imbalance that still survives between the sexes in science, we need to see how it was created and where it originated. Modern scientific organisations have developed from ones that existed earlier. Examining the past can help us realise how we have arrived at where we are today – and the whole point of doing that is to make sure that everybody enjoys a better future.

PAST

Past

If ever thou purpose to be a good wife, and to live comfortably, set downe this with thy selfe: Mine husband is my super-iour, my better; *he hath authority and rule over mee* ...

William Whately, *The Bride Bush*, 1617

NAMES ARE IMPORTANT. When Mr and Mrs Nighting-ale's baby daughter was born in Italy in 1820, they called her Florence, because that was where she was born (her sister was named after Naples). **Florence Nightingale** grew up to become the Lady of the Lamp, Victorian England's most famous nurse. Although she had no children, she did have a pet owl, of which she was enormously fond. She decided to call her Athene.

Why did Florence Nightingale choose to give her beloved owl the name of a Greek goddess? Trad-itionally owls are wise birds, and in ancient Greece Athene was the goddess of wisdom. According to Greek mythology, she was Jupiter's daughter, and was born by springing out of his head already dressed in battle armour. Athene – often known by her Roman name of Minerva – became an important symbol of learning.

Athene is easy to recognise because she is always

shown with her owl, her books and her helmet. This picture (Figure 1) is the frontispiece of an encyclopaedia that was published in the early 19th century. Athene's owl is perched on top of her helmet, and she is holding a military spear in her right hand. With her left arm, she is pointing to the shelves of books, which she has revealed by pulling back a heavy curtain. Athene is telling a student that books – and in particular, this new encyclopaedia – are the best route to knowledge.

Unsurprisingly, the student is male. At that time, girls weren't supposed to spend their time reading scientific books. Instead, they were being taught how to sing, cook and sew. When a girl grew up, she was given away by her father to her husband, and was expected to dedicate her life to his. Athene represented knowledge, but it was men who were meant to acquire it.

Although this picture was published in 1817, almost 200 years ago, its basic message is not so very different from the Nobel Prize medals that are awarded nowadays. Women appear on these medals (Figure 2, page 24), but very rarely win them. In principle, both men and women are eligible, but in the entire 20th century, only five women were awarded the physics and chemistry prizes, compared with several hundred men. Nature stands on the left, scantily clothed and clutching an overflowing horn (or cornucopia) of fruit and grains. The other woman, Science, is pulling a veil away from Nature's face to symbolise how scientists uncover the hidden secrets of the natural world. Until very recently, these scientists were overwhelmingly male, and the Latin inscription

FIGURE 1 *Minerva directing study to the attainment of Universal Knowledge. Frontispiece of* The New Encyclopædia, *1807*

FIGURE 2 *Nobel Prize medal for chemistry and physics*

round the edge reads 'How good it is that man's life should be enriched by the arts he has invented'.

Scientists Anonymous tells the stories of real women – not symbolic ones – who participated in scientific research and helped to make science so important today. Most versions of science's past leave women out as if they had never existed. But women were there – you just have to look carefully and choose the right places to search.

I wrote this book to convince readers – boys as well as girls – that the past provides a valuable pathway into the future. But before I started, I had to make an important decision: *What should I call the women I wanted to write about?* This is a crucial question because historians should respect people from the past. Women were often literally owned by their men – they were given their father's surname when they were born, and their husband's when they got married. So I wanted to give them names to represent their own identity. But what is the best way of doing that?

The British 20th-century chemist **Dorothy Hodgkin** illustrates my dilemma. The only name that is truly hers is Dorothy. However, male scientists are referred to by their surnames – we talk about Newton not Isaac, Darwin not Charles and Einstein not Albert. So I believe that to call her Dorothy would be patronising and would re-inforce the idea that women scientists somehow do a different sort of science from men. So perhaps I should use her childhood surname, Crowfoot? But that would also be insulting: she chose to call herself Hodgkin after she got married, so what right do I have to call her something different?

These questions about names have no right answers, but in this book I will call women by the surname they themselves used, whichever man it originally belonged to. I hope that the women I describe – Florence Nightingale, Dorothy Hodgkin and many more – would have approved.

In the past, girls were trained to attract a good

husband and run the home, so they learnt how to sew, clean and cook. In richer homes with servants, daughters were allowed to read and study, but they had to sit quietly and stay inside while their brothers enjoyed themselves or went off to university. They had little choice about what to learn. Science was for boys, and any girl who liked science was regarded as an oddity.

Women's education has improved because of repeated campaigns waged mostly – but not entirely – by women. Men used to boast that they were the cleverer as well as the stronger sex, and insisted that God had created women to look after them and their children. Fortunately for women living now, some people protested against this view. One of the earliest English campaigners for female education was Bathsua Makin, who struggled against oppression in the 17th century. 'Had God intended women only as a finer sort of cattle,' she argued, 'He would not have made them reasonable.' Since then, Makin's successors have hammered home the same message – girls can think and they should be educated.

Nowadays many girls continue their education after they leave school, but in the past, intelligent women were considered abnormal. In the 18th century, women were still advising their daughters to conceal their cleverness in order to avoid being laughed at. The famous writer Samuel Johnson summed up what many men felt: 'It's like a dog walking on his hind legs', remarked Johnson about a woman making a speech – 'It is not done well, but you are surprised to find it done at all.'

Even at the end of the 19th century, the entrance qualification for one English girls' school was being able to
sew a buttonhole, and many men remained totally
opposed to female education. But by then, feminist
campaigners were starting to succeed in their demands
that women should be able to have good schools and
go to university.

During the 1970s, members of the Women's
Liberation Movement continued the fight to make
women feel free, so that they could improve life for
themselves as well as for future generations. The Eagles,
a famous American pop group of the time, urged women
to break through the social barriers that held them cap-
tive. 'We live our life in chains', they sang, 'And we never
know we hold the key.' For the first time, huge numbers
of women found the courage to unlock the gates of
their psychological prisons and demand the same privi-
leges as men.

A century ago, Hertha Ayrton protested that 'The
idea of "woman and science" is completely irrelevant'.
Hopefully, by the time another century has gone by her
wish will have come true, and there will be no need for
books like *Scientists Anonymous*.

The 17th Century: Patrons, Parents and Partners

The 17th Century: Patrons, Parents and Partners

Frailty, thy name is woman!
William Shakespeare, *Hamlet,* 1601

D ECIDING WHERE TO start a book is very difficult. Lewis Carroll knew how hard it can be.

'Where shall I begin, please your Majesty?', asked the White Rabbit. Alice listened closely for the answer. *'Begin at the beginning,'* the King said, gravely, *'and go on till you come to the end: then stop'.*

Of course, as Alice realised, it's not that easy: you have to choose where to begin. Unlike a war or the reign of a monarch, there is no definite date for the origin of science. Many people claim that science first appeared in Greece around 2,500 years ago, but that leaves out the Babylonians and the Egyptians who came before them. Another possibility is to say that science began in 1543, when Copernicus put the sun instead of the earth at the centre of the universe, but it was at least another century before most people accepted such a revolutionary idea.

Since historians disagree, I was forced to make my

31

own choice. I decided to start this book in the 17th century, because that's when the earliest scientific societies were established.

Scientific Societies

For Strength is increased by Exercise, Wit is lost for want of
Conversation ... Wherefore, my Advice is, we should imitate
Men, so will our Bodies and Minds appear more Mascu-
line, and our power will increase by our Actions.

Margaret Cavendish, *Orations of Divers Sorts*, 1662

T HE WORLD'S FIRST major scientific institution was
London's Royal Society. It was founded in 1660,
when Charles II came to the throne after the Civil War
and the rule of Oliver Cromwell. Starting with Paris,
other cities followed England's example, and by the
end of the century there was a network of scientific
societies spread out across Europe.

These early scientific societies were important
because they enabled gentlemen to exchange ideas
with each other. Before that, groups of friends did meet
to discuss science in each other's homes, but there were
no national organisations. The Royal Society's first
members included young, enthusiastic men who later
became famous, including Christopher Wren (the
architect of St Paul's cathedral), the chemist Robert
Boyle (who gave his name to the law about gases) and

Robert Hooke (a brilliant microscopist who accused Isaac Newton of stealing his ideas).

The period from around 1550 to 1700 is often called the Scientific Revolution, because this was when reformers successfully campaigned for a new type of learning. They argued that the best way to find out about the world is to carry out experiments, not to rely on books that were hundreds of years old. The new scientific societies were set up to advertise this new approach to nature.

Before the Scientific Revolution, there had been two major sources of knowledge: Aristotle, the Greek philosopher who taught that the planets revolve around the earth in circles; and the Bible, which people interpreted as God's own words. By the end of the revolution, these were both regarded far more critically. Everybody believed that the sun lies at the centre of the universe, and scientific investigators had invented accurate instruments to explore the world by observing, measuring and testing it. New scientific societies were encouraging research as well as communicating discoveries and ideas all over Europe. They were just as important as the universities: although Isaac Newton was a Cambridge professor, it was London's Royal Society that published his great book on mechanics and gravity.

There were virtually no women in these scientific societies. Men regarded women as being intellectually inferior – their job was to run the home and bring up children, not engage in academic debates. In any case,

compared with nowadays, very few people were educated, and there were many, many intelligent women
who never even learned to read and write, let alone prove
a geometrical theorem or watch a chemical reaction.
However, some wealthy women did find opportunities
to practise science. The most famous example of these
enterprising and unusual women is Margaret Cavendish.

The First Woman at the Royal Society

Margaret Cavendish (1623–73) could study science
because she was rich. She waited on the Queen and
married the wealthy Duke of Newcastle, who paid for
her books to be published and introduced her to his
scientific friends. During the Civil War they lived in
Paris, along with many other supporters of the royal
family, which gave Cavendish the opportunity of meeting some of Europe's leading scholars, such as René
Descartes, Newton's French rival (Cartesian coordi-
nates are named after Descartes).

Cavendish was in Paris before the Royal Societies of
London and Paris had been created, when people discussed scientific ideas at home. Dinners were long serious
affairs, and scientific debates took place around the
table. In the picture on page 36 (Figure 3), Cavendish is
sitting at the head of the table next to her husband.
Such conversations meant that women as well as men
could learn about the latest ideas, and when they
returned to England the Cavendishes took continental
theories back with them.

FIGURE 3 *Margaret Cavendish (Duchess of Newcastle) and her family.*
Frontispiece of Margaret Cavendish, Natures Pictures Drawn by
Fancies Pencil to the Life *(London, for J. Martin and J. Allestyre,*
1656). Original by Abraham van Diepenbeke, engraved by Peter Clouwet

Cavendish was a very outspoken woman who antagonised people by writing critical books. One victim of
her attacks was the Royal Society's leading experimenter, Robert Boyle. What's the point, she asked, of
looking at a bee through a microscope if you can't
make it produce more honey? And if you're so clever,
why can't you build a honeycomb? Not surprisingly,
Boyle was furious at being ordered to lay on some
entertaining experiments when she demanded to visit
the Royal Society in 1667. The lecture room was packed
that day, because many of the Fellows – including the
diarist Samuel Pepys – wanted to see this eccentric
woman in her extravagant clothes. Contemptuously,
they called her 'Mad Madge'.

This nickname is still used by many people today, but
it is very insulting, and a good example of how easy it is
to mock women who were fighting against the conven-
tions of their time. Cavendish was certainly unusual,
but that does not mean she was mad; even though some
of her ideas were old-fashioned, she also made valid
criticisms.

Some writers defend Cavendish by calling her 'the
first feminist scientist', but that is also misleading. It simply doesn't work to look back into the past and describe
men and women with modern labels like 'feminist' or
'scientist'. We have to be sympathetic to ideas of the
period: people who lived centuries ago were no more
stupid than people are now, and theories that seem out-
landish to us often described the world quite well.

By our standards, Cavendish was not a feminist.

Although she complained bitterly about the lack of education for girls, like most of her contemporaries she believed that women were born less able to carry out intellectual work than men. Experts of the time still followed Aristotle's opinion that the sexes have different types of brain – men's are hot, dry and good for thinking with, whereas women's are cold and wet, which makes them emotional rather than rational creatures.

Elevating Cavendish to the status of scientist is also wrong. She wrote in a rambling style, carried out no original experiments, and nobody took her ideas very seriously. Even more importantly – and this may sound a strange thing to say – there were NO scientists during the 17th century. For one thing, the word wasn't invented until 1833, so even men like Isaac Newton weren't scientists but natural philosophers. Unlike modern scientists, natural philosophers had no large laboratories to work in, and no salaries or research grants. Still odder from our point of view, they believed their research would help them learn more about God. Religion was central to natural philosophy, although it is now a separate subject from modern science.

Nowadays, being elected to a country's national Science Society is like receiving a knighthood: it is one of the highest honours a scientist can receive. Scientists benefit enormously from belonging to one of these prestigious groups. They can discuss the latest research before it is even published, they are in a strong position to get funding for their next project, and they can influence their government's science policy.

Very few women are invited to join these privileged clubs: London's Royal Society has over 1,200 Fellows, but only about 4 per cent of them are women. The picture is very similar in other countries.

Why are there still so few women in the world's top societies? One answer is that there are not many high-calibre female scientists to pick from. Many people refuse to appoint women of a lower standard simply to make the numbers look better. Women want to be promoted because of their excellence, not because they happen to be female. They want to be regarded as exceptional scientists, not unusual women.

Another way of thinking about this question is to look at the past and recognise that societies were traditionally all-male organisations. The Royal Society was founded by wealthy men who didn't even bother to exclude women officially – they just *assumed* that women would not be interested. The Fellows were taken by surprise when Margaret Cavendish demanded to attend a meeting, and afterwards they decided to close ranks and formally ban women. The first female Fellows were not elected until 1945, when 89 per cent of the votes were in favour of the biochemist Marjory Stephenson and the crystallographer Kathleen Lonsdale. But British scientists were not exceptionally prejudiced – for the next 40 years London's Royal Society had a higher percentage of female Fellows than the USA's National Academy of Sciences.

Patrons

The Countess of Pembroke was the greatest patronesse of witt and learning of any lady in her time. She was a great chemist and spent yearly a great deale in that study. She kept for her laborator in the house Adrian Gilbert ... She also gave an honourable yearly pension to Dr. Mouffett, who hath writt a booke De insectis. *Also one Boston, a good chemist.*

John Aubrey, *Brief Lives*, c. 1693

A s well as banning women from their meetings, the Royal Society effectively excluded men who were not rich enough to fund their own experiments. Modern scientists earn salaries by working for large organisations such as universities, industrial companies or governments. But in the past there were no paid scientific jobs, and experimenters had to find their own sources of money. They searched for wealthy patrons who would sponsor their research. Some of these wealthy backers were women, who exerted a strong influence on science by deciding which men to support.

For centuries, the most powerful female patrons were queens and princesses. Even though they could not go to university themselves, they often supported scholars. Elizabeth I is England's most famous example. Her favourite experimenter was John Dee, who married one of her ladies-in-waiting. Dee was a mathematician who specialised in practical subjects, such as navigation and geography. Queen Elizabeth sometimes rode over to his large, rambling house with its enormous library and rooms full of instruments. Although Dee died 50 years before the Royal Society was founded, through Elizabeth's backing he became one of Europe's leading researchers.

Other Elizabethan aristocrats acted as patrons on a smaller scale. Mary Herbert, the Countess of Pembroke, was an exceptionally learned woman. She wrote and translated her own books, as well as sponsoring hopeful young authors and funding expeditions to America. Still more unusually, she was fascinated by chemistry, and she had several long-term house guests – including a close friend of John Dee – who carried out their research at her expense. In return, they taught her the latest ideas and showed her how to do experiments.

Patronage always worked in two directions. Both people gave something, but both people also gained. Without receiving financial support, many men would have been unable to develop their ideas, and science would have suffered. But the women who gave the money also profited, because by paying lecturers to teach them, they could buy the education they craved. In addition, in their books grateful authors wrote lavish acknowledgements to their wealthy patrons, who then acquired the reputation of being intellectual women with deeper interests than clothes, children and card games.

Royal families were linked to one another by marriage, and they continued to control many of Europe's finest scholars. Several princesses patronised Gottfried Leibniz, the famous German mathematician and philosopher. Although Leibniz became a member of London's Royal Society in 1673, to earn his living he worked (much against his will) as the Prince of Hanover's librarian. Leibniz was protected by a network of powerful women, including the Prince's wife and daughter, who made Leibniz the first President of the Berlin Academy of Sciences. When the Hanover family took over the British throne, Princess Caroline defended Leibniz against his great enemy, Isaac Newton. It now seems clear that without the help of these royal women, Leibniz would not have been able to develop theories which lie at the heart of modern mathematics.

Naturally, only a few women were in a position to dispense large amounts of money. One particularly important patron was **Queen Christina of Sweden**, a very outspoken woman who gathered some of Europe's cleverest men together in her palace at Stockholm. In contrast, **Anne Conway** was a shy recluse, a semi-invalid living in rural England, yet she too knew eminent 17th-century scholars. Although neither of these women could join official scientific societies, they both set up informal discussion circles based in their own homes.

Wealthy female patrons led fascinating lives. Learning about them is important because their influence spread not just over their own time but also stretched forward into the future. Without their involvement, science would have developed very differently.

A Royal Athene

Queen Christina of Sweden (1622–89) was celebrated all over Europe as the Athene of the north. Artists imagined her in armour like the original Athene, wearing an elaborate helmet on her head and accompanied by an owl perching on a pile of books. Because Christina was rich, she could pay scholars to visit her in Stockholm and so she made her palace an academic centre. Christina benefited twice over from these guests. She studied with them instead of going to university, and she boosted her prestige and power. Paris and London were the leading cities of the world, but she wanted them to have a new rival – Stockholm.

Christina's most important scientific visitor was France's leading intellectual, René Descartes. Descartes is now celebrated as a great philosopher, but he also carried out many scientific experiments, was interested in medicine and introduced new mathematical ideas. Christina spent almost three years persuading Descartes to make the long voyage north, and he eventually agreed because he wanted her to act as patron for another clever woman, his friend Princess Elisabeth of Bohemia.

Christina had a formidable reputation, although it is difficult to be absolutely sure how true some of the stories about her are. She was supposedly brought up like a boy, and had no interest in clothes or gossiping with other women. Apparently she only needed five hours sleep a night, and had three major interests – horse-riding, studying and politics.

When Descartes arrived, she set up a strict timetable for him to teach her: five hours of lessons three times a week, starting at 5 o'clock in the morning. At that time of day it was still dark, and it turned out to be the coldest winter for 60 years. Descartes had never encountered such harsh conditions, and after a couple of weeks he fell ill and died.

After Descartes's death, Christina seems to have lost her interest in science and concentrated on more traditional subjects, such as Greek and Latin literature. Five years later, she created an international scandal by converting to Catholicism (Sweden was strongly Protestant) and then abdicating from the throne.

Historians still argue about the relationship between Christina and Descartes. Did she behave like a siren, luring him to his death? Or did he corrupt Christina and lead her to abandon her religion and her crown? Like many questions in history, there's no right answer – it depends on how you want to interpret the evidence.

An Aristocratic Scholar

Anne Conway (1631–79) was a brilliant woman who spent most of her life trapped in men's houses – first her father's and then her aristocratic husband's. Because she suffered from crippling headaches, she was a semi-invalid who led a quiet life. Instead of travelling or throwing parties like other wealthy wives, Conway invited eminent scholars to visit her large country home, Ragley Hall, so that she could join in their discussions of the latest scientific and medical ideas. She wrote a book on scientific philosophy, and scholars throughout Europe admired her work. As Leibniz commented, Conway was an 'extraordinary Woman'.

Anne Conway adored her elder brother. After he went away to Cambridge University, he sent her books so that she could study by herself at home, and he introduced her to one of his tutors, the famous philosopher Henry More. Conway and More became close friends, and he often went to stay with her at Ragley Hall, where he taught her about philosophy. But this was not a simple teacher-pupil relationship. She developed her own ideas, different from his, and their debates influenced his own books. More dedicated one of them to Conway, gushing in the flowery language that authors used for thanking aristocrats: 'in the knowledge of things as well Natural as Divine you have not only outgone all of your own Sexe, but even of that other also'. In other words, she had outstripped men as well as women.

England's most famous doctors repeatedly tried to cure Conway's headaches, but they got worse rather than better. The physicians used her as a case-study to develop new ideas about how the body and the mind are linked together. Many people believed that men and women had different types of brain, and they thought that Conway suffered so much pain because she was a woman who studied too hard. More took her to Paris, where the surgeons wanted to bore a hole in her skull to release the excess vapours pressing on her brain. Fortunately for her, they decided to release some blood from her arteries instead.

When they got back to England, More persuaded Europe's leading medical alchemist, Francis Mercury van Helmont, to examine Conway. He stayed for nine years, living at her expense. Although van Helmont failed to cure Conway's headaches, together they studied ancient texts and debated one of the oldest philosophical problems: is there just one kind of substance in the world, or are people's minds made up of something different from their bodies and other solid objects? Conway knew how much her physical pain affected her thoughts and her emotions, and she argued that everything is composed of a single fundamental substance.

When Conway was 47, she became even sicker than before. Her husband was away in Ireland and refused to come back, so More and van Helmont cared for Conway while she was dying. To commemorate this woman who had been a close friend as well as a patron, they published her small book on science and philosophy – an exceptional achievement for a 17th-century woman.

Female Artisans

To buy Wool and Flax, to die Scarlet and Purple, requires skill in Natural Philosophy. To consider a Field, the quantity and quality, requires knowledge in Geometry. To plant a Vineyard, requires understanding in Husbandry: She could not Merchandise, without knowledge in Arithmetic: She could not Govern so great a Family well, without knowledge in Politics and Economics: She could not look well to the ways of her Household, except she understood Physic and Chirurgery.

Bathsua Makin, *An Essay to Revive the Antient Education of Gentlewomen*, 1673

CRAFT WORKERS WERE vital for the development of science in the 17th century. Metal working, glass blowing and other traditional techniques were essential for making the new instruments that were being invented, while artists were needed to draw biological specimens, diagrams and maps. Ordinary working people were skilled at activities that now seem scientific but were then part of daily life. For instance, women collected herbs to make medicines, farmers predicted the weather accurately and miners developed chemical processes for producing metals from ores.

47

The women in artisan families were unusually powerful. In some ways, they were better off than wealthy aristocratic women who were essentially owned by their husbands. Craft workshops were run as family businesses,
and women not only shared the work, but also played a
prominent managerial role. They learnt how to make
instruments and supervise financial transactions. Girls
as well as boys were taken on as apprentices, and daughters were trained by their fathers. When they were fully
qualified, women often either married the owners of
other shops or else took over the family affairs when
the man of the household died.

Craft knowledge was handed down in families, to
daughters as well as to sons. **Maria Sibylla Merian** was
apprenticed to her father, a well-known artist and
engraver. Because she had learned how to look very
closely at what she was drawing, she was later able to
transfer this skill and observe insects in great detail.
Unusually for a woman, she became a famous insect-
collector, an entomologist who studied insects as well as
illustrating them.

Modern scientific equipment is produced in large
factories, but instruments used to be made by skilled
craft workers running their own small businesses. They
adapted traditional methods going back over centuries
in order to make new types of instruments for scientific
research. For example, opticians making reading-
glasses also produced early microscopes and telescopes,
while ship outfitters who were compass experts started
to make accurate magnetic equipment.

This craft tradition lasted for a particularly long time in Germany. Maria Eimmart is an interesting example. Her father ran an astronomical observatory, and was also head of an art academy. From him, she learnt how to draw as well as how to look at the stars. Combining her two skills, she made 250 careful drawings of the moon, which formed the basis of a new lunar map. She married a physics teacher, but – like so many women – she died in childbirth when she was very young. However, through her, her husband inherited her father's observatory.

Modern astronomical instruments are controlled by computers, but old-fashioned telescopes needed two people – one to look at the night sky, and the other to write down the observations. Many sisters, daughters and wives were roped in to help, and some of them became skilled astronomers in their own right. **Elisabetha Hevelius** is particularly fascinating, because pictures in her husband's book show them working together as a team.

Between 1650 and 1710 an astonishing 14 per cent of German astronomers were women. One of the most famous was **Maria Winkelmann**, who married an astronomer and eventually ran her own observatory, where she taught her children. However, it was very hard for a female astronomer to combine her scientific work with looking after her home and family. When the German astronomer Maria Cunitz published a book of astronomical tables in 1650, people simply assumed that her husband had done the work. Even men who praised her also criticised her for ignoring her family. One writer fumed: 'She was so deeply involved in astronomical calculations that she neglected her household. She spent most of the day in bed because she had tired herself out watching the stars at night.'

As Cunitz found, all the credit usually went to the man of the household. Another good example is Margaret Flamsteed, who was married to England's Astronomer Royal, John Flamsteed, at the end of the 17th century. She became his apprentice, and – like other astronomical wives – she worked closely with her husband. After his death, she collected all their readings together, but she published them under his name: like so many other scientific women, her activities have been concealed behind those of a famous man.

Back in the 17th century, the modern scientific disciplines had not yet been established. For example, pharmacology is now an academic science, but at that time traditional skills and customs were extremely important. For centuries, women had been treating their families and dispensing herbal medicines. Although they were not formally as well-educated as male physicians who had been to university, they had an enormous amount of practical expertise. In any case, before powerful drugs and antiseptics were introduced, doctors were incapable of curing many illnesses and just had to help their patients die comfortably.

Women were the experts in one particularly important aspect of medical care: obstetrics, looking after women during pregnancy and childbirth. Pregnant women now receive medical treatment as if they were ill. But before the 19th century, university-trained male doctors were rarely involved. Instead, female midwives were responsible for looking after the mothers before, during and after the birth. They often passed on their experience directly by training assistants rather than by writing textbooks, so most of them have disappeared leaving little trace behind them. One exception was **Louise Bourgeois**, whose manual on childbirth makes it clear how expert these vanished women were.

An Intrepid Collector

Like other girls in artistic families, **Maria Sibylla Merian** (1647–1717) was trained at home. However, unlike young men, she had no opportunity to travel from one workshop to another and learn different skills. But Merian was an exceptionally adventurous woman who started to travel in her forties, even though at that time most women of her age had either died in childbirth or were regarded as being too old to do anything interesting. First Merian left Germany to settle in Amsterdam. Later she embarked on a trip that would have been extraordinary for a man let alone a woman – she spent two years in Surinam, a Dutch colony in South America, observing insects and plants.

Throughout her childhood, Merian was taught how to be an artist. As well as being good at drawing, she had to learn practical skills, such as mixing colours together or engraving designs on to copper plates ready for printing. She married one of the other apprentices, but decided not to follow the normal route of working as her new husband's partner. Instead, she set up her own business selling luxurious cloth painted with flowers, and she employed female apprentices to help her.

Merian's first book was about caterpillars. This was an important subject because German manufacturers wanted to find a cheap replacement for Chinese silkworms. She drew fine detailed pictures showing the life cycle of many different insects as they developed from eggs into butterflies. For her second book, on flowers, she invented a new printing technique to produce bright and realistic colours.

After twenty years, Merian left her husband and went to live in an experimental religious community. There she shared the communal tasks of baking bread and weaving cloth, but she also studied hard, learning Latin and examining plants and insects. When she moved to Amsterdam ten years later, Merian supported herself by illustrating scientific textbooks. But she was determined to go to Surinam so that she could observe the behaviour of live insects rather than just investigate dead ones in museum collections.

At last Merian managed to save up enough money, and with one of her daughters she set off for Surinam, a risky voyage lasting several weeks. She gathered insects and plants in the cool mornings, and then observed and painted them later on. She knew that she would need to recoup her costs when she got back to Amsterdam, and she preserved crocodiles, snakes and iguanas in brandy so that she could sell them to rich collectors. She also earned money for her beautiful pictures.

While Merian was in Surinam, the rich Dutch planters mocked her for her unusual behaviour. Unlike other natural historians, she was interested in how plants were used, and she asked the local people about recipes and medicines. She criticised the planters for treating the Indians badly, reporting that slaves were committing suicide and killing their own children because they were forced to work in such intolerable conditions.

However, it was not the arrogant Europeans but the climate that forced Merian to leave Surinam and return to Amsterdam, where she published her greatest book, on the wildlife of Surinam. It was lavishly illustrated, and showed European naturalists plants and insects they had never encountered before. Men all over Europe admired her work, and the Czar of Russia even hung her portrait in his study.

As a good craftswoman, Merian ensured that she passed her skills on to her family by training her daughters, who helped her complete her famous book. Natural historians thought so highly of her work that they paid her high compliments: six plants, nine butterflies and two beetles were named after her.

A Rooftop Astronomer

Elisabetha Hevelius (1647–93) always longed to study astronomy. When she was sixteen, she seized her opportunity – she married Johannes Hevelius, a rich and famous astronomer who was more than three times her age. He owned a large brewery in Gdansk (then called Danzig), an important port on the Polish coast, and he built a large observatory on the roof of his house.

There is very little written information about Elisabetha Hevelius. We know that she had four children (one of whom died), was good at maths and Latin, and that her husband nursed her devotedly during an attack of smallpox that permanently scarred her face. He must have been an exceptional man, because he declared that 'women are definitely just as well suited to observing as men'.

Most unusually, three large pictures were published showing her working as her husband's astronomical partner (Figure 4). Two people were needed to operate the enormous brass instruments used for measuring star angles, and Elisabetha was the person Johannes trusted most. When an English rival came to inspect their equipment, she was given the task of demonstrating how accurate their readings were.

After Johannes Hevelius died, Elisabetha was left to run the brewery by herself and produce their star catalogue. She published it under his name, and it became the definitive map of the stars for the next 100 years. Although Elisabetha Hevelius was famous for her astronomical expertise all over Europe, her memorial is hard to see – far away on the planet Venus a small crater has been named after her.

FIGURE 4 *Elisabetha and Johannes Hevelius observing with their great sextant. Johannes Hevelius,* Machina cœlestis *(Danzig, 1673)*

An Astronomical Marriage

When she was young, **Maria Winkelmann** (1670–1720) found being a girl very frustrating. She was fascinated by astronomy, but knew that it was impossible for her to go to university. Instead, she found two men to teach her. The first was a local farmer who had astonished professional astronomers by discovering a new comet. The second man, Gottfried Kirch, was much older than her but was Germany's most distinguished astronomer at the Berlin Academy. After a long fight with her parents, she gained their permission to marry him.

Kirch had learnt his astronomy in two ways. He had gained practical experience as an apprentice in an observatory, and he had learnt theoretical and mathematical astronomy by going to university. But for Winkelmann, a woman, university was not an option.

By choosing Kirch as her husband, Winkelmann gained the opportunity of working with an expert, but she was also responsible for looking after the household and the children. The husband and wife worked side by side as a team, sometimes dividing the two halves of the sky between them, sometimes working in shifts so that they could cover the whole night. One night he was asleep when she observed a new comet, but it was announced as his discovery.

Although Winkelmann shared Kirch's work for many years, after he died the Academy refused to give her his job and forced her to leave the home where they had observed together. She worked in other observatories, and gradually rose to become a master astronomer with apprentices of her own. She also trained her children, two girls and a boy. Like his father – but not his mother or sisters – the boy studied at university as well as being apprenticed in an observatory. Winkelmann realised that there was only one way for her to get back into the Berlin Academy – as an assistant to her own son, who inherited his father's job and later employed his two sisters.

A Royal Midwife

In the 17th century, men were physicians and surgeons, while women were nurses and midwives; men wrote technical books, while women carried out the practical work. **Louise Bourgeois** (1563–1636) was one of the first women to break down those barriers – she was a midwife who wrote a theoretical textbook, and included information about the male specialities of medicine and surgery.

Bourgeois grew up in a wealthy Paris suburb, and was – by the standards of the time – well-educated for a woman. Her husband worked for one of France's leading surgeons, and so she had good opportunities to learn about anatomy. However, as a woman, she decided to study midwifery. First she practised on poor people (her patients presumably thought it was better to have a student than nobody). Because Bourgeois had such influential medical contacts, after she qualified she became the midwife for many rich and aristocratic people. She attended thousands of births, but her most important client was the Queen, who paid her for seven deliveries – 1,000 ducats for a son but only 600 for a daughter.

By the time that she was 40, Bourgeois had reached the peak of her profession. But then she went further. She wrote a comprehensive textbook which not only gave instructions about coping with normal births, but also taught midwives about anatomy and physiology, topics usually reserved for men. She suggested what to do if things went wrong, and explained how to prevent problems in advance by resting and eating properly – all routine advice now, but she was one of the first to emphasise its importance.

When the Queen was deciding whether to employ Bourgeois, she relied on recommendations from her friends but also insisted on seeing the midwife for herself. In the 16th century appearance was very important because people believed that your looks revealed your character. Bourgeois paid great attention to her picture at the front of her book (Figure 5). Her velvet cap and gold cross advertised that she worked for the Queen. Her wide shoulders showed her strength, an important qualification for a midwife; her tranquil expression indicated that she would remain calm in any crisis.

Bourgeois's book was translated into other languages, and many writers plagiarised it by incorporating long sections into their own manuals. This meant that Bourgeois improved midwifery all over Europe, not just in France. For another couple of hundred years, women remained the childbirth experts.

En ce parfait tableau le defaut de peinture
Se congnoist aujourdhuy clairement a nos yeux
Pource qu'on n'y peut veoir que du corps la figure
Non l'esprit admiré pour chef d'oeuure des cieux

S. Hacquin

FIGURE 5 *Louise Bourgeois. Frontispiece of Louise Bourgeois,* Observations diverses sur la sterilité, perte de fruit, foecondité, accouchements et maladies des femmes et enfants nouveaux naiz, *1609*

Enlightenment Dilemmas: Duty versus Disobedience

Enlightenment Dilemmas: Duty versus Disobedience

[My granddaughter should] *conceal whatever learning she attains, with as much solicitude as she would hide crookedness or lameness; the parade of it can only serve to draw on her the envy, and consequently the most inveterate hatred, of all he and she fools, which will certainly be at least three parts in four of all her acquaintance.*

Lady Mary Wortley Montagu, letter to her
daughter, 1753

THE 18TH CENTURY is often called the Age of Reason, because that was when philosophers declared that the best way to solve the world's mysteries is not to read the Bible, but to think clearly, carry out experiments and apply abstract mathematical theories to the real world. They encouraged people to work things out for themselves rather than believe what they had read in books. This period is also known as the Enlightenment, since writers who liked metaphors proclaimed that the bright light of reason had pierced through the dark clouds of superstition and ignorance: in other words, to see is to understand.

The scientific societies that had been established in the 17th century continued to expand, and during the Enlightenment it became fashionable for women as well as men to buy scientific books. Inventors introduced new instruments that could measure far more accurately than ever before, and they started using mathematics for analysing the vast numbers of observations they collected. Popular lecturers travelled round Europe and the east coast of America demonstrating the latest equipment, such as electrical machines with flashing lights and sparks, or microscopes that could magnify tiny wriggling organisms on to a large screen. As experimenters advertised the power of science to transform people's lives, governments started to pour money into scientific research.

The Industrial Revolution started in England, where wealthy landowners set up factories using the latest technology – such as steam engines – to make them run more efficiently. As the country became richer, the population grew not only in London, but also in the new northern cities set up near the natural resources of coal, iron and water. England was often at war with France, where the emphasis on science and reason exploded in 1789, the year of the French Revolution. Broadcasting their famous slogan 'Liberty, Equality and Fraternity', the citizens of Paris overthrew the monarchy and founded modern democratic Europe.

However, 'Fraternity' means 'Brotherhood', which leaves out half the human race. As George Orwell put it in his book *Animal Farm*, 'All animals are equal, but some are more equal than others.' Even though science became more and more important during the Enlightenment, women had to struggle for their right – their liberty and their equality – to learn about it.

The Age of Newton

The most beautiful Woman in the World would not be half so beautiful, if she was as great a Mathematician as Sir Isaac Newton ... While she was contemplating the Regularity of the Motions of the heavenly Bodies, very irregular would be the Proceedings of her Children and Servants; the more she saw of Order and Harmony above, the more Confusion and Disorder would she occasion in her domestic Affairs below; the more abstracted she was in her Ideas and Speculations, the greater Stranger would she be to the Rules and maxims of common Prudence.

Gentleman's Magazine, 1738

A S WELL AS being called the Enlightenment, the 18th century is often known as 'the age of Newton'. Although Newton himself died in 1727, during the following decades natural philosophers in Europe and America explored his ideas and developed them further. Newton wrote on many different topics, but his two most important books were on gravity and light.

According to scientific mythology, science changed for ever when Newton was inspired by watching an apple fall from a tree. This is an attractive story, but Newton's success did not come overnight. He spent years checking his results before he published his great book, *The Mathematical Principles of Natural Philosophy*, in 1687. Newton declared that the force of gravity operates throughout the universe, so the planets circling the sun obey the same mathematical laws as an apple falling from a tree. Because he insisted that most of the universe is empty space, many people disliked his theories – his critics refused to believe that gravity can travel through a vacuum with nothing to carry it along. Resistance to Newton was especially strong in France, where René Descartes remained science's great national hero until the second half of the 18th century.

Another reason why Newton's ideas were not immediately accepted is that they were hard to understand: brilliant scholars are not always good at explaining their ideas clearly. Newton revolutionised the world of physics, yet he deliberately made his book about gravity so difficult that very few people would be able to understand it. He did not, he told a friend, want to be pestered 'by little Smatterers in Mathematics'. Newton's theories only became generally accepted after other people had deciphered and interpreted his complicated writings.

Language was also a problem. Newton originally wrote his *Natural Philosophy* in Latin (which is why it's often called the *Principia*), and the first translation into English only appeared after he had died. But language wasn't the only obstacle: even in English, the mathematics was very challenging. Students needed to start with easier versions, and authors wrote textbooks with simplified explanations to make the mathematics and the physics clearer.

Two major stages are involved in communicating scientific results around the world: translation from one language to another, and interpretation into understandable terms. Both these steps are vital for scientific progress, since without transmitting new ideas, the same research would have to be repeated time after time in different places.

These two processes were often carried out by women, who found translating and interpreting to be ideal work. Although they were banned from universities and public laboratories, they could study at home and fit in their writing between other jobs, such as looking after their children and their husbands.

Women were vital for passing scientific knowledge from one place to another, and from one generation to the next. But they were not just neutral transmitters – women also changed science because they expressed their own opinions. The first person to translate Newton's great book on gravity into French was a woman, **Émilie du Châtelet**. In fact, until the end of the 20th century, hers was the only French translation of Newton. However, it was far more than a straightforward translation, since she also explained, tested and criticised Newton's theories.

Another woman who helped to spread Newton's new ideas throughout Europe was **Laura Bassi**. Italy was a major exception to the general rule of excluding women from universities during the 18th century, and Bassi became a professor of physics.

Women are supposed to be very bad at mathematics,

but both du Châtelet and Bassi grappled successfully with Newtonian geometry and calculus. One advantage of mathematics (at least, before electronic computers were invented) is that you don't need a laboratory with expensive instruments; provided you think carefully, you can manage with a pencil and paper. This made it easier for women to study mathematics at home. Astronomers who were trying to verify Newton's predictions had to carry out complicated calculations by hand, and they often asked their wives and daughters to help them. These women were called 'computers', because they computed, or worked out, the mathematical formulae that predicted when comets would appear or where to look for a new planet.

Some Enlightenment men did recognise that women are capable of carrying out mathematical work competently and efficiently. In 1709, the editor of a very popular magazine for women (called *The Ladies' Diary*) followed his readers' advice about what they wanted. The circulation soared after he got rid of all the recipes, and put in more mathematical problems. This journal's success shows that women can be just as enthusiastic about maths as men – and just as good.

Newton's French Interpreter

Émilie du Châtelet (1706–49) was tall and beautiful. Many scientific women would object to being described by their looks, but du Châtelet was extremely concerned about her appearance. She loved clothes, dancing and entertaining, and she spent a small fortune on decorating her house. But at the same time, she was a dedicated scholar. When she had to meet a deadline, she scarcely slept, plunging her hands into ice-cold water to keep herself awake. She believed that the most important thing in life is to be happy, and she was as enthusiastic about her work as her pleasure.

Luckily for du Châtelet, her father was rich and unconventional. Instead of sending his clever daughter to a convent school, he decided that she should be taught at home and given the sort of education that was more typical for boys than for girls. She was free to browse in her father's large library, and could apparently speak six languages when she was only twelve years old. At that time few children – even brilliant boys – learnt any science, but du Châtelet resented not being able to pursue the same career as a man. She was determined to carve out a good position for herself. Women, she wrote, should study 'to console them for everything which makes them dependent on men'.

Du Châtelet was 27 years old when she started studying mathematics and Newtonian physics. By then, she was married to a rich aristocrat and had two children. She was also falling in love with another man, Voltaire, France's most famous author who wrote plays, essays and satirical novels such as Candide. With her husband's agreement, Voltaire and du Châtelet lived together for fifteen years in her large country house at Cirey. They organised the house so that they each had separate apartments where they could write. In addition to collecting 21,000 books for their enormous library, they bought scientific instruments for carrying out experiments. She took over the large hall, testing Newton's theories with wooden balls swinging from the rafters. At other times, she hid away in her study – thinking, writing and endlessly rewriting.

Together du Châtelet and Voltaire wrote France's first main book on Newton's physics. *Elements of Newton's Philosophy* might not sound an exciting title, but the book was very controversial because accepting that Newton was right meant agreeing that Descartes, France's great scientific hero, was wrong. Written in clear, simple French, this book explained Newton's theories about gravity and light so that ordinary people could understand them. Their joint publication was a big success, and is often seen as a turning point in French physics, when people switched from Descartes to Newton. But, surprise, surprise – only Voltaire's name was on the title page! However, the book did include a long poem by Voltaire paying tribute to Émilie du Châtelet as a great genius who studied at his side.

Her next scientific project was even more ambitious: a comprehensive textbook on physics explaining the relationships between the theories of Newton, Descartes and Leibniz. Du Châtelet worked in complete secrecy because she was frightened of being laughed at for undertaking such a massive project. Like many women, she published her book anonymously. This meant that when she got good reviews, she knew they were fair.

Although du Châtelet longed to continue working, she kept getting sidetracked by problems connected with Voltaire, their house and her children. Since she had already translated some non-scientific books into French, she decided to tackle Newton's book on gravity, the *Principia*. Du Châtelet's work was constantly being interrupted, but it was thorough. As well as reading all three Latin editions of the *Principia*, she studied the latest English, Dutch and French attempts to develop Newton's work further. She included discussions of this new research in her long comments, so that the French version of Newton's *Principia* was more comprehensive and up-to-date than anything available in English.

While she was involved in this massive project, du Châtelet discovered that she was pregnant. Because she was convinced that she was going to die, she worked harder and harder, sometimes as much as eighteen hours a day. Her gloomy predictions turned out to be right, and she died a few days after her baby was born. Because she had published many books and scientific pamphlets, du Châtelet was famous as France's 'illustrious female scholar', and some of her mathematical friends arranged for her French version of the *Principia* to be published. Many people still found it hard to believe that a woman could be a scientific star. Voltaire remarked that 'she was a great man whose only fault was being a woman. A woman who translated and explained Newton ... in one word, a very great man.'

An Italian Professor

In most countries, being a woman made it impossible to study at university, let alone teach. Yet **Laura Bassi** (1711–78) was only 21 years old when she started lecturing on physics at the University of Bologna, and in 1776 she became Europe's first female professor. Bassi was, of course, exceptionally clever, but she also benefited from being swept up in a campaign to advertise Italy as a modern, liberated country.

Bassi's father was a wealthy lawyer who loved showing off his precocious daughter, and he encouraged his friends to give her private lessons in science and maths as well as in literature and languages. He then encouraged her to undergo a gruelling series of debates with eminent scholars. These took place in front of large audiences – not just lecturers and students, but also city governors, the Archbishop and an assortment of curious onlookers. Rather like a royal occasion, these public performances were organised with great ceremony. They were designed to impress the world that Bologna was an exceptionally advanced city. One visitor wrote, 'All the gentleman of Bologna make a great display of this girl, and depict her everywhere as the miracle of our age'.

Very few of Bassi's lectures have survived, so although she became famous all over Europe, we know little about her work. She did publish four papers on the physics of air and liquids, but her activities as a teacher and experimenter were more important. The most modern scientific theories had been produced by Newton, and they were still very controversial. Italy seemed to be behind England and France, and because Bassi taught Newtonian physics, she helped to improve Italy's scientific reputation. Physics had previously been a very theoretical subject, and she insisted on carrying out experiments, just as Newton had recommended.

Bassi was valuable to Bologna as a symbol of female freedom, but she was not treated in the same way as the male lecturers. She was paid less money, she was given less teaching to do, and she was expected to stay at home and look after her children. For 40 years, she struggled to improve her position to benefit not only herself but also the situation of other female scholars.

When the professor of experimental physics died in 1772, she decided to wage one more battle. She applied for the job and won it after four years of arguments. Ironically, she was perhaps too successful: when conservative men realised how many rules she had changed, they decided not to admit women to the university in the future.

Science at Home

*The Dressing-Room, not the Study, is the Lady's Province –
and a Woman makes as ridiculous a Figure, poring over
Globes, or thro' a Telescope, as a Man would with a Pair of
Preservers mending Lace.*

James Miller, *Humours of Oxford*, 1730

IT IS OFTEN hard to draw definite boundaries
between what was and wasn't science. Take the
Duchess of Portland, an extremely rich Enlightenment
woman who found a marvellous way to spend her fortune – she collected strange, beautiful objects such as
shells, rocks and plants, and classified them into different arrangements. This passion first started when James
Cook gave her some shells after one of his voyages to
Australia. By the time she died in 1785, the Duchess's
collection was so enormous that the auction to sell it off
lasted for 38 days. Famous natural historians bought
rare specimens to examine, many of which ended up in
museums.

Was the Duchess of Portland a scientific collector?
Many women (and men) liked to accumulate curious
objects, but she was doing far more than just amusing
herself with a hobby. In earlier centuries, the distinc-

tions between science and non-science were not clear-cut, and many women were involved in activities that would nowadays be called scientific. Before large towns and railways developed, most people lived in isolated places far from shops and doctors. Women were often responsible not only for cooking, cleaning and caring for the children, but also for treating illnesses, growing food efficiently and preparing chemicals such as dyes and preservatives. There was no firm division between this traditional practical expertise and the knowledge that would later become classified into scientific disciplines – pharmacology, agriculture, botany, chemistry.

Women's lives centred closely round their own homes – or to be more accurate, their fathers' or their husbands' homes. Some girls were lucky enough to have indulgent fathers who let them join their brothers while they were being taught by tutors. But when the boys went off to boarding school and university, the girls were left behind. Very little information about these girls survives, but – like the tips of icebergs – snippets of evidence do remain.

One good example is Elizabeth Tollet, an Enlightenment poet who complained about being criticised for sharing her brothers' lessons:

> *Is this a crime? for female Minds to share*
> *The early Influence of instructive care?*

Tollet excelled at physics and mathematics, yet she had to stay behind at home while her far less clever brothers went to university. Like many sisters, she was left alone with only her books for company.

What cruel laws depress the female Kind,
To humble Cares and servile tasks confin'd?

When Tollet expressed her own anger, she knew that she was speaking on behalf of many other frustrated girls who might have become eminent scientists if they had been born 300 years later.

Elizabeth Tollet was not the only woman who objected to her secondary status in life. During the 18th century, more and more women tried to exert their independence, and some of them published books demanding better education. Many of them adopted pen names because they were frightened of being identified. The anonymous 'Sophie' gave her book a resounding title – *Woman not Inferior to Man.* She protested that men like to maintain their power over women by keeping them ignorant and then describing them as stupid. She wrote: 'The Men, by thinking us incapable of improving our intellects, have entirely thrown us out of all the advantages of education and thereby contributed as much as possible to make us the senseless creatures they represent us.'

Sophie and her sister campaigners started to be successful, and men published books so that girls like Tollet could learn about science at home. To make their books more interesting, these authors set up imaginary conversations between an ignorant pupil and a wise teacher, such as a sister and an older brother who had been to university. These fictional girls often asked silly questions, while the boys claimed to know all the right answers. Pictures showed the girl listening obediently while the boy told her what to look at: here (Figure 6) a student is teaching his younger sister about electrical machines, which were then very new and exciting.

Female campaigners became increasingly aggressive during the 18th century. The most famous was Mary Wollstonecraft, who is now often called 'the first feminist'. In her book *A Vindication of the Rights of Woman* (1792), she demanded that women should be given a better education. She argued that it is wrong for women not to be taught properly, because that meant they were 'treated as a kind of subordinate beings'. According to Wollstonecraft, many women were inherently more intelligent than their husbands, which explained why they were often the true rulers of the household. She wrote in an inflammatory style that 'the most salutary effects tending to improve mankind might be expected from a REVOLUTION in female manners'.

Unsurprisingly, Wollstonecraft had to endure many insults – one man even called her a 'hyena in petticoats'. Even so, by the end of the Enlightenment women were reading scientific books and going to public lectures. Although some men encouraged their interest, others were very critical. One cynic sneered that 'some score of them had their tablets and pencils,

FIGURE 6 *Euphrosyne learns about electricity. Benjamin Martin,*
The young gentlemen's and ladies philosophy *(2 vols, London,*
1759–63)

busily noting down what they heard, as topics for the next conversation party'. He was accusing women of wanting to impress people with their superficial knowledge, but perhaps he was worried that women would outsmart him?

Women themselves started to teach girls about science (Figure 7). Margaret Bryan ran several schools in southern England as well as publishing books on physics and astronomy. One picture shows her sitting with two of her pupils as though they all belonged to a family. In contrast with boys' books, Bryan emphasised that science was a gentle activity for girls to carry out at home. Other women wrote similar books for different scientific subjects, such as chemistry and botany – and many boys borrowed their sisters' books.

Nowadays, scientists' children usually know very little about what their parents do, because they work away from home in offices and laboratories. But during the 18th century, the situation was very different, because most science was done at home. This meant that daughters, wives and sisters were inevitably involved in experiments being carried out around them.

Women were particularly important in sciences like chemistry and astronomy, which need at least one person to do the experiments or make the observations, and another person to write them down. The most famous astronomical couple were **Caroline Herschel** and her brother William, who came over to England as musicians, but ended by dedicating their lives to their shared obsession with science.

FIGURE 7 *Mrs Bryan with two girls. Frontispiece of* Margaret Bryan, A
compendious system of astronomy *(1797). Engraving by W. Nutter
from a 1797 miniature by Samuel Shelley*

Intellectual women enjoyed more freedom in
France than in England. Wealthy women ran *salons* –
social gatherings – in their own homes where the latest
books and scientific ideas were discussed. Although

81

women were not regarded as men's equals, wives were expected to help their husbands so that they worked together as a team. The most famous scientific wife was **Marie Paulze Lavoisier**, who joined in her husband's chemical experiments and whose diagrams were vital for his revolutionary book on chemistry.

Sweeping the Skies

At first sight, **Caroline Herschel** (1750–1848) seems to be an excellent example of a neglected scientific pioneer. She discovered several comets, spent years perfecting complicated mathematical calculations and won the praise of astronomers all over Europe. Yet nowadays very few people have heard of her. Is this simply because she was a woman, or are there other reasons why she is so little celebrated?

Herschel herself provided a clue. 'I am nothing, I have done nothing,' she wrote, 'a well-trained puppy-dog would have done as much'. She thought of herself as her brother's humble assistant, and often denied that she had done any more than follow his orders. This picture (Figure 8) shows her offering a cup of tea to sustain William, who scarcely seems to notice her as he busily polishes a mirror for his telescope. In her biography, Caroline described how she looked after her 'brother when polishing, since by way of keeping him alive I was constantly obliged to feed him by putting the victuals by bits in his mouth … serving tea and supper without interrupting the work with which he was engaged'.

Caroline Herschel.

FIGURE 8 *Caroline and William Herschel. Coloured lithograph after Alfred Diethe, c. 1896.*

Was William a cruel man who made Caroline his slave? That's too simple an answer. The situation was more complicated because – like many women – Caroline regarded herself as being inferior to men. She helped to put herself into a subordinate position. Caroline Herschel revolved around her elder brother William like a planet around the sun – they worked as a team but she was happy to take a dependent role.

As a child in Germany, Caroline Herschel's ambition was to sing. Her father wanted her to be educated with her brothers, but her mother insisted that because she was a girl, she should learn how to do housework. She dreamed of escaping from her mother and studying music with William, who was living in England. And when she was fifteen, that was exactly what happened: William rescued her and took her to Bath.

At first, her new life seemed marvellous. She studied English, started to train as a professional singer and enjoyed looking after the older brother she adored. But gradually, his interest in astronomy started to take over both their lives and she gave up any idea of establishing her own career. All she wanted to do was help William, who earned money as a musician, but whose passion was astronomy.

Together they spent every spare minute making telescopes. Caroline had many of the worst jobs, such as sieving horse manure to make a smooth bed for large mirrors. But she was also responsible for recording observations and carrying out calculations, and they both often worked right through the night. After

William became famous for discovering the planet Uranus, the King gave him a salary. At last they had enough money to devote all their time to astronomy, and they bought a house near the royal castle at Windsor.

The Herschels converted their house and garden into a giant astronomical observatory. Because they made enormous telescopes, they could see distant stars that had previously been invisible. When a telescope tube was lying on the ground waiting to be pointed up towards the sky, the King persuaded the Archbishop of Canterbury to crawl through it, exclaiming 'Come, my Lord Bishop, I will show you the way to Heaven!'

Caroline Herschel worked harder and harder. One dark night she slipped in the snow and tore open her leg on a meat hook, but she tried to ignore her injury and continue with her astronomical observations. Although she dedicated herself to making her brother famous, she remained behind the scenes. She was desperately shy and was embarrassed by her German accent, so she rarely said anything in public.

After fifteen years of near-slavery, she did receive some recognition. The King gave her a small salary, so for the first time ever she had money of her own to spend. She was thrilled. However, there was a downside: her brother was getting married, and she could no longer share her life with him. Although she was very lonely, she now had more time to spend on astronomy. She studied the stars methodically with a special small telescope called a sweeper, and found eight new comets. Three of her reports were published in the Royal Society's journal. For the first time, the Society officially recognised that a woman could make valuable contributions to science. Nevertheless, they refused to let her enter the meeting rooms, let alone make her a Fellow.

By now Caroline was famous in her own right, but she still took on tedious tasks for William, such as compiling a list of mistakes in older star catalogues. Caroline Herschel lived to be almost 100 years old, yet her life had only one theme: 'All I am, all I know, I owe to my brother; I am only the tool which he shaped to his use.'

A Revolutionary Chemist

Marie Paulze (1758–1836) was only thirteen years old when she rejected her first suitor – a man of 50 – and agreed to marry Antoine Lavoisier, an ambitious lawyer. She found herself in charge of a Parisian household, and the wife of a wealthy businessman who was obsessed by chemistry and geology. Lavoisier followed a rigorous schedule: science from six to nine in the mornings, a full day of meetings and then back into the laboratory for three hours after dinner. Although Marie Paulze Lavoisier (the double surname she herself used) was so young, she immediately started learning chemistry, English and Latin so that she could share her husband's research. For over twenty years they worked and travelled together.

86

Lavoisier wanted to revolutionise chemistry, and he introduced the names, symbols and equations that chemists still use today. Like modern scientists, Lavoisier insisted that numbers and precise measurements were vital for chemistry, and he invented instruments to measure small weights extremely accurately. Important research was also being carried out in England, and because Paulze Lavoisier had learned English, she could translate books and articles into French for her husband. This meant that she, too, was aware of the latest chemical controversies, and so she could collaborate with Lavoisier in his research. Together they entertained some of the world's most famous chemists.

As well as chemistry, Lavoisier wanted to revolutionise society. He owned a large farm where he carried out agricultural experiments, trying to improve the quantity as well as the quality of the wheat, milk and meat his farmers produced. Although he was very rich, he wanted to help the peasants who worked for him to lead a better life. He tried to persuade the government to change the laws so that ordinary workers would be better off. Paulze Lavoisier shared his political beliefs, and she toured round factories and farms with him, searching for ways of making the peasants' work more profitable.

Paulze Lavoisier loved drawing, and she took lessons from one of Paris's most famous artists, who painted a splendid double portrait of Marie and Antoine Lavoisier. It shows one version of how they lived and worked together (Figure 9). He is sitting at a table writing his revolutionary book on chemistry, and his new experimental equipment is laid out on the table and the floor. But Paulze Lavoisier was important in her own right, and she dominates the centre of the picture. Her husband is gazing up at her as though asking for guidance. Behind her, a large portfolio of her own art is lying across a chair.

In contrast, her drawings of their laboratory (Figure 10, page 90) present a different picture. They show how she took part in his experiments. She drew herself sitting at a table, writing down the results as he calls them out – a vital task. In addition, Paulze Lavoisier was responsible for looking after the experimental records and organising the laboratory.

She also drew the diagrams for Lavoisier's textbook. The importance of precise measurements was one of the central planks of Lavoisier's new chemistry, and Paulze Lavoiser invented new ways of drawing scientific apparatus so that other experimenters could copy it exactly. Her careful illustrations were crucial for the success of Lavoisier's book, and she established a new standard for scientific diagrams.

Lavoisier genuinely wanted to improve the appalling conditions endured by the peasants. However, during the Reign of Terror after the French Revolution, he was accused of being an idle aristocrat who got rich at the expense of the workers. Along with his father-in-law, he was taken to prison and Paulze Lavoisier visited regularly. Although she tried to rescue them, they were both guillotined. She was devastated, and even spent two months in prison herself.

FIGURE 9 *Marie Paulze and her husband Antoine Lavoisier. Jacques-Louis David, 1788*

After Paulze Lavoisier was released, she spent years trying to get back all their confiscated property. She also wanted to restore her husband's reputation, and she published the papers he had been working on

Lavoisier dans son laboratoire

Expériences sur la respiration de l'homme exécutant un travail

FIGURE 10 *Marie Paulze Lavoisier: her sketch of the laboratory. Marie Paulze Lavoisier, Experiments on the respiration of a man carrying out work, probably 1790–91.*

while he was in prison. For many years, she invited distinguished writers, artists and chemists to her house for dinners and discussions every week. Her guests remembered the Reign of Terror, and so had to be very careful about saying anything controversial. At her parties, they were free to say what they really believed. As one grateful visitor exclaimed, 'You have to have lived under the vacuum pump to appreciate the luxury of breathing'.

In Disguise

I have been led to imagine that the few extraordinary women who have rushed in eccentrical directions out of the orbit prescribed to their sex, were male spirits, confined by mistake in female frames.

Mary Wollstonecraft, *A Vindication of the Rights of Women*, 1792

THE AMAZONS WERE a mythical group of women warriors who set up their own state (definitely not a kingdom!) ruled by a queen. All men were banned, and these fierce women cut off their right breasts so that they could draw back the strings of their bows to shoot arrows. Although these mutilated fighters never actually existed, they are an inspiring symbol for women who yearn for adventure and want to run their own lives.

By disguising themselves as men, some women behaved as though they were real-life Amazons. Catalina de Erauso escaped from a Spanish convent and for twenty years enjoyed being a bandit instead of a nun. She sailed to South America, enlisted as a soldier and killed her own brother in a duel. Christian Davies from Dublin behaved very differently: she loved her husband so much that when he went missing in Flanders during a battle, she transformed herself into a soldier and went searching for him; successfully passing herself off as a man, she eventually found him after thirteen years – and later died in Chelsea Pensioners' Hospital for soldiers. The Enlightenment's most famous cross-dressers are Anne Bonny and Mary Read. They signed up as pirates and toured the Caribbean plundering ships; when they were arrested, they both escaped the gallows by becoming pregnant.

When women wanted to enter the male world of science, one solution was to dress in disguise. Some of the ones we know about – such as the botanical explorer **Jeanne Baret** and the French mathematician **Sophie Germain** – managed to hide their true identity for a surprisingly long time, so probably there were others who were never found out. These cross-dressing women could escape detection because clothing for the two sexes used to be completely different. Three hundred years ago, trousers automatically indicated that the wearer was a man, and there was no need to look very closely. Now that it is easy for a woman to dress like a man it is more difficult for her to disguise herself: when everyone dresses similarly, you have to pay far more attention to people's shape and posture to work out which sex they are.

A Seafaring Botanist

Jeanne Baret (1740–1816) was the first woman to sail right round the world, but she did so disguised as a man called Bonnefoy. All the way from France to Tahiti, only one other person on the ship knew that Bonnefoy was really a woman – her employer, Philibert Commerson, a doctor who was collecting plants and animals for the French king.

Not surprisingly, members of the crew were suspicious of this beardless young man who only washed or undressed in secret. How did she manage to avoid detection? Commerson was just as keen as Baret to maintain her disguise. According to naval tradition, women on board ship brought bad luck, and the punishment for disobeying the ban was high – officers were suspended for a month, and ordinary sailors were sentenced to 15 days in chains. Baret bandaged her breasts to flatten them, and she and Commerson often hid themselves away in his cabin, supposedly suffering from sea-sickness.

Baret also disguised herself by working hard at jobs usually reserved for men. She was Commerson's botanical assistant, and he paid her to collect plants as well as to illustrate them. When Commerson climbed up snow-covered hills to collect rare plants, Baret followed close behind him, carrying all their food, weapons and scientific equipment. According to one report, Bonnefoy 'worked like a negro' (at that time, many people made disparaging remarks about non-Europeans who, like women, were regarded as inferior). As a tribute to her expertise, Commerson dedicated a new plant genus to her – Baretia.

Because the Tahitians knew little about French fashions, they could see more clearly that Baret's body looked like a woman's rather than a man's. The secret came out halfway across the Pacific Ocean, when Tahitian islanders ran after her shouting 'ayenene, ayenene' ('girl, girl'). After the captain took her back to the ship, Baret confessed to her crime. She explained that as an orphan, she found it easier to support herself dressed as a man – and she had jumped at the chance of a voyage round the world. From then on, she carried loaded pistols to protect herself against attackers.

However, it does seem likely that before then, Commerson's colleagues had decided to turn a blind eye and ignore the unorthodox situation. Neither Commerson nor Baret were punished, and she continued working with him on his natural history collections until he died. The French Navy called her an 'extraordinary woman' and even granted her an annual pension.

Mathematical Transformations

Sophie Germain (1776–1831) was an enormously gifted mathematician who was born at the wrong time and in the wrong family. As a child she was obsessed with maths, but her father was so horrified at such an unfeminine passion that he confiscated her candles and put out the fire in her room to prevent her from studying. The ink froze, but still she worked, wrapped up in her bedclothes. Faced with this determination, her father gave in, but for many years she had to learn alone from books.

When Germain was eighteen, a new scientific training college (the École Polytechnique) opened in Paris.

Although as a woman she was banned from entering the building, she took over the identity of another student, Antoine-August le Blanc, who had found the work too difficult. Long after the real le Blanc had left Paris, the college went on sending him lecture notes and problem sheets, which Germain submitted under his name. This trick worked for a couple of months, until one of the lecturers wondered how le Blanc had suddenly transformed himself from an appallingly bad student into an amazingly clever one. He summoned le Blanc to his office, and was astonished to meet Sophie Germain. Instead of dismissing her, he encouraged her to develop her mathematical skills.

Germain started carrying out her own research into number theory, a specialised branch of mathematics. Hiding behind her old pseudonym of le Blanc, for several years she corresponded with a leading expert. At first he had no inkling of her true identity, and as they exchanged ideas, she laid the foundations for discoveries not completed until the late 20th century. Later she became fascinated by physics experiments with vibrating plates, and she developed mathematical theories to explain the results. However, she was always hampered by her lack of formal training.

In 1816, Germain anonymously entered a competition set by the Paris Academy of Sciences, and she won the top prize. Still more importantly, she became the first woman allowed to attend the Academy's meetings. At last, she could meet top-class mathematicians without hiding behind a man's name.

The Victorian Age:
Initiative and Independence

The Victorian Age: Initiative and Independence

The chief distinction in the intellectual powers of the two sexes is shown by man's attaining to a higher eminence, in whatever he takes up, than can woman – whether requiring deep thought, reason, or imagination, or merely the use of the senses or hands.

Charles Darwin, *The Descent of Man, and Selection in Relation to Sex,* 1871

SCIENCE AND INDUSTRY grew together during the 19th century. Industrialisation was strongest in Britain. New machines had been optimistically introduced during the Enlightenment, but they transformed workers – including women and young children – into miserable automatons who slaved for long hours yet earned very little money. But as the poor became poorer, the rich became richer, and privileged Victorians boasted about the booming economy and the rapidly expanding British Empire.

Developing from its Enlightenment foundations, science became increasingly important. During the 1830s, two new words were invented that gave experimenters a status they had never before enjoyed – 'scientist' and 'physicist'. New universities were built to cater for the growing population, and they included large laboratories for teaching not only traditional subjects such as physics, astronomy and chemistry, but also new scientific disciplines – biology, geology and anthropology. Scientists searched for mathematical laws to unify the universe, and governments, as well as private entrepreneurs, poured money into scientific research and exploration.

For the first time, being a scientist was a career option for a young man who had not been born into a wealthy family. A blacksmith's son – Michael Faraday – became the world's leading expert on electromagnetism and President of the Royal Institution. Before then, it would have been impossible for a boy from such a humble background to reach the peak of professional science, yet Faraday's inventions led to the electrical equipment that transformed the world.

Even though it remained unthinkable for a woman to achieve such an eminent position as Faraday, some women did contribute greatly to science's growth. Long after he became famous, Faraday still praised his first teacher, who was called Jane Marcet. She was an extraordinarily successful writer, a Swiss woman who settled in London with her husband, a doctor. Although she never claimed to be a scientist herself, Marcet wrote introductory books that were translated and published in many countries.

Faraday first encountered science in Marcet's *Conversations on Chemistry*, which sold many, many thousands of copies. Our modern electrical industry depends on the discoveries Faraday made during the 19th century, and he always acknowledged Marcet's vital influence.

Women's Networks

We meet you in "Society" with crowds of friends about & in an atmosphere of finery & artificiality. Suppose I, or any woman – let her be as fascinating as possible – were to bombard you with scientific talk – would you not rather go off to the stupidest little girl who had not a thought above her pretty frock, than begin a discussion?

Eliza Linton to Thomas Henry Huxley, 1868

JUST AS IN the Enlightenment, women became involved in science because research was still taking place in private homes. They participated in work usually credited to their fathers, brothers and husbands. Take the case of Charles Darwin, Victorian England's most famous scientist, who spent most of his life working at his secluded house in a remote country village. Like all husbands at that time, he relied on his wife Emma to run his house and bring up their large family. Darwin was often ill, and then he demanded extra care and attention. Sometimes he behaved like a child himself. Once he wrote in a letter to her, 'Oh Mammy I do long to be with you & under your protection for then I feel safe.' On top of all that, he expected Emma and his children, along with their friends and relatives, to help him with his experiments.

Darwin's science occupied the entire household. His children were so used to their father's strange obsessions that when one of his sons visited a friend's home, he politely enquired where the barnacle dissecting room was. When Darwin wanted to investigate a carnivorous plant's feeding habits, he took over one of the kitchen shelves as a laboratory and scoured the house for flies and spiders. Sometimes he treated the children and their pets as though they belonged to his experiments. He sketched their expressions and made scientific notes on their rate of development. Like any proud father, he admired his son Francis playing the flute – but he was also analysing the shape of Francis's mouth and comparing it with an ape's.

While he was preparing his great book on evolution, Darwin recruited women to help him. As well as discussing his ideas with Emma, he enlisted other men's wives to translate foreign articles and also to edit his own writing, so that ordinary readers could understand him. But although Darwin relied on women for help, in his books he declared that they were born intellectually inferior to men. His theory of evolution was extremely influential, and Darwin was said to have provided scientific proof confirming what people had believed for centuries: however hard women worked, they were doomed by their sex never to achieve as much as men.

Victorian scientists chose their wives carefully; they wanted women who could help them with their work as well as look after them. Isolated in rural Ireland, the mathematician George Boole wrote to a friend that 'there is absolutely no person in this country except my wife with whom I can ever speak on subjects like this'. Mary Boole was so well-educated in logic that she provided an in valuable intellectual sparring partner, but it was her husband who became famous.

Other talented and dedicated 19th-century women shared Mary Boole's fate. Many of Darwin's friends married scientists' daughters, who had already been trained by their fathers to carry out scientific work. The famous geologist Charles Lyell adopted this tactic. He was a social climber who met many of London's most eminent scientists through marrying into the right family. For his success, he depended on his wife, **Mary Lyell**, yet only his name appears on the title pages of the books which she helped him to write.

Through such marriages, famous men of science were related to one another in extended scholarly networks that resembled royal dynasties. The women in these scientific families were well-educated, clever and influential. One of them reported that an eminent scientist's wife 'was an amiable accomplished woman, drew prettily & what was rare at the time had studied science, especially geology and it was chiefly owing to her example that her husband turned his mind to those pursuits in which he afterwards obtained such distinction'.

As well as exerting hidden power over their menfolk, these talented women communicated with each other. Excluded from official scientific organisations and universities, they formed their own intellectual circles, exchanging news about discoveries and giving each other emotional support. **Mary Somerville**, a brilliant mathematical physicist, met and wrote to many other scientific women. One of her close friends, **Ada Lovelace**, was an expert mathematician and an expert on early computers. Computer programming is now predominantly a male world, but it was a woman – Ada Lovelace – who first outlined the principles.

These women made vital contributions to the future as well as to Victorian science.

A Geological Expert

Mary Lyell (1808–73) and her husband Charles were devoted to each other, yet even before they were married, he made sure that she would be useful for his career. He was an ambitious lawyer who wanted to become a geologist. Because his fiancée's father was a distinguished London scientist, Charles Lyell gained the opportunity to meet many influential people. He persuaded his future bride to study geology so that she could share his ideas, and also to learn German so that he would not have to bother.

Once they were married, she became even more indispensable to her husband. For their honeymoon, they went on a geological field trip! They never had any children, and Charles Lyell regarded his wife's time as his own. He was the world's most famous geologist during the 19th century, yet he depended on a woman whose importance he never fully acknowledged. Darwin was one of Lyell's most enthusiastic admirers, but even he disapproved of his friend's behaviour towards his wife. In a letter to his own wife, Emma, Darwin boasted: 'I want practice in ill-treating the female sex. I did not observe Lyell had any compunctions.'

Mary Lyell made up for several of her husband's deficiencies. Because he was bad at languages (or too lazy to learn them?), she translated foreign books and letters into English for him. Because he had poor eyesight, she read aloud to him for hours on end. Because he could not draw well, she illustrated the rocks and other items they collected together. And there are no prizes for guessing who undertook the tedious work of sorting, classifying and labelling the geological collection which grew so enormous that they had to move to a larger house.

In addition, at her husband's request, Mary Lyell became an expert on shells. Geologists often need to identify fossil shells so that they can work out the age of the rocks they are studying. Mary Lyell took over this vital part of her husband's scientific research. When she found she needed an assistant to help organise her shell collection, she recruited her maid Antonia. She wrote to her sister, 'I have taught Antonia to kill snails and clean out the shells and she is very expert'. It seems that in the Lyell household, everyone was swept up in Charles's passion for geology.

A Scientific Queen

Victorians called **Mary Somerville** (1780–1872) the 'Queen of 19th-century Science' because she published excellently clear books explaining complicated ideas in mathematics and physics. However, like many women, she lacked confidence in her own ability. According to the biological theories of the time, women were inferior to men, and Somerville was ready to criticise herself. 'I have perseverance and intelligence but no genius', she remarked; 'that spark from heaven is not granted to the sex'. Her work suggests otherwise – she was obviously an extremely clever woman. Who knows what she could have achieved if she had been given better opportunities?

When Somerville was young she was fascinated by mathematics, but because that was seen as a boy's subject she had to study in secret in case her father found out. She escaped by marrying her cousin, a sympathetic doctor who encouraged her research. After they moved south to London from their original home in Scotland, Somerville became friendly with eminent scientific men from Britain and abroad, and she discussed her ideas with them.

Her first scientific article, about her research into sunlight, was so impressive that the Royal Society published it; however, her husband had to present it for her because no women were allowed in the meeting rooms. Soon Somerville was asked to translate and explain a complicated French book on physics, but – always self-critical – she worried whether she would be able to do it well enough. She agreed on one condition – if her manuscript was no good, then it would be burnt. Somerville worked in her room alone, snatching time between looking after her house and family. 'Frequently,' she wrote, 'I hid my papers as soon as the bell announced a visitor, lest anyone should discover my secret'.

In spite of her anxiety, Somerville's book – *The Mechanism of the Heavens* – was so successful that it became the standard textbook on mathematical astronomy for the next 100 years. Later she published more books and articles, and became famous throughout Europe. She went on studying right up to her death, and Oxford University named one of its first women's colleges after her.

But although she won many medals, Somerville was never allowed to join the Royal Society. The Fellows compromised by placing a marble bust of her in the entrance hall. However, this was a symbolic tribute that did little to change scientists' attitudes. On the contrary, it probably provided a convenient excuse so that the Society could avoid discussing the problem.

The First Computer Programmer

Ada Lovelace (1815–52) never met her father, the famous poet Lord Byron. However, her overbearing mother encouraged Ada's flair for mathematics by ensuring that she was taught up to university standard at home. With her mother's backing, a succession of tutors forced Lovelace to work harder and harder, sometimes inflicting harsh punishments. Even after she was married, her mother organised her family and her home.

Throughout her life, Lovelace was often ill. When she was a teenager, she had to lie in bed for three years and then walk on crutches. She suffered many physical problems, and they were made worse by psychological difficulties. Like other Victorian woman, she found it hard to cope with being regarded as strange because she was clever. She got married when she was twenty, and went to live in the country where she could read and study. She had three children, but found that the more she studied mathematics, the less she could bear to be with them.

As an aristocratic young woman, Lovelace met many eminent people, including famous scientists. She was only seventeen when she first met Charles Babbage, a Cambridge maths professor, who became one of her closest friends. They wrote long letters to each other about mathematics and logic. Babbage designed several large calculating machines, and Lovelace became involved in his most ambitious project, an Analytical Engine.

Babbage wanted his Engine to produce mathematical tables of numbers (such as logarithms) to be used by astronomers and other scientists. At that time, long, tedious calculations were being carried out by people – women as well as men – called computers. Babbage dreamed of making a machine to replace all this human labour. His Engine would, he claimed, be quick, cheap and would not make mistakes. He planned to make it from columns of rotating metal cogs, all powered by steam. Because he had failed to finish building an earlier device, Babbage found it hard to get funding.

When a French article appeared about his Analytical Engine, Lovelace translated it into English. Babbage was delighted, but asked her 'why she had not herself written an original paper on a subject with which she was so intimately acquainted?' She decided to write her own commentary, and as she became more absorbed in the subject, her 'Notes' stretched to become three times as long as the original paper. She persuaded her husband to help by giving him secretarial tasks – the reverse of how married couples usually worked together!

The ideas that Lovelace introduced would later revolutionise computing. Her outstanding innovation was the concept of computer programming. She borrowed the idea from a French tapestry maker who used stiff cards with holes punched in them to control weaving patterns. Lovelace described how these Jacquard cards could be used to tell a calculating machine what to do. As she put it, 'the Analytical Engine weaves algebraic patterns just as the Jacquard-loom weaves flowers and leaves'. When electronic computers were invented in the 20th century, programming instructions were fed in on punched cards as Lovelace had suggested.

In some ways Lovelace was even more of a visionary dreamer than Babbage. He was only interested in using his Engine to manipulate numbers, but she discussed how machines might be programmed to generate music. She did, however, make it absolutely clear that the Analytical Engine could not be creative. Its job, she wrote, 'is to assist us in making available what we are already acquainted with'.

Lovelace's notes were published under the initials AAL – enough for her friends to recognise the author. She thrived on their praise, but within a few months she became depressed and ill. With no scientific project to work on, she started drinking and gambling. Her health deteriorated, she experienced terrible pain, and she died of cancer when she was only 36 years old.

And Babbage's Engine? It was never built, but remained a set of drawings accompanied by Ada Lovelace's 'Notes'. Although a working replica has been made for London's Science Museum, Babbage's suggestions had little direct influence on modern computers. However, Lovelace's suggestion of programming seemed so important that the language ADA was named after her.

Spreading the Word

Needle-work and intellectual improvement are naturally in a state of warfare.
Sempronia (Mary Lamb's pen-name), *British Lady's Magazine*, 1814

VICTORIAN WOMEN DID enjoy recognition in one scientific role – popularising the research of famous men. Writing introductory books was looked down on as a job suitable only for women, who were said to be incapable of producing their own ideas, but (sometimes) clever enough to understand those of men.

There are two main objections to these low opinions of writing and of women. For one thing, scientific progress depends on making new ideas accessible to everyone so that the next generation of researchers can build on earlier results. Science cannot proceed without a shared fund of knowledge. Just as importantly, many women did far more than simply water down complicated theories – they criticised, corrected and interpreted the books they were explaining and translating. One excellent example is **Clémence Royer**, who provided the first French translation of Charles Darwin's book on evolution. She disagreed with some of his ideas about women's inferiority – and she said so (much to his annoyance).

Women were essential for the growth of science. They made themselves indispensable by taking advantage of their traditional female skills, especially drawing and languages. They illustrated, translated and explained scientific books, tasks that might sound secondary but that are essential for progress. Without women, the whole pace of scientific change would have slowed down. Many experiments would never even have been finished, let alone been recorded properly and tidied up for publication. In addition, new scientific ideas would have taken far longer to spread to other countries and laboratories, and might never have reached the students who needed to learn in order to take science further.

However clever and knowledgeable they were, women were not allowed to join the ranks of professional scientists, but were regarded as second-class amateurs. This distinction was particularly noticeable in astronomy. There were many excellent female astronomers, including **Agnes Clerke** from Ireland and **Maria Mitchell** in America. Although they made important and original contributions, they were not treated in the same way as male scientists.

Even rich women were limited in what they could achieve because their behaviour was restricted, especially during the first half of the century. They were simply not allowed to go on strenuous collecting expeditions or join scientific societies. In some ways less-privileged women were better off. **Mary Anning** came from a poor family and had very little formal education, but because her father had taught her how to clamber over dangerous rocks she found some of Britain's greatest fossils, which enabled male scientists to discover more about evolution.

A French Feminist

According to Charles Darwin, **Clémence Royer** (1830–1902) was the 'oddest and cleverest woman in France'. Many French people agreed, which is why in 1881 she was included in a cartoon series called 'Today's Men' (Figure 11). The caricaturist has shown her writing her most recent book, *Welfare and the Moral Law.*

Royer was one of France's leading feminists in the 19th century, an unconventional and outspoken woman. She published several books on politics as well as science, but she was most famous – or notorious – for her French translation of Darwin's book on evolution, *The Origin of Species,* because she added her own opinionated preface and notes explaining why she thought Darwin was wrong to claim that women are less clever than men. 'Woman is the one animal in all creation about which man knows the least', she declared. Darwin was extremely angry, because her intervention encouraged French people to condemn his theories.

Royer had an unsettled childhood. After her father became involved in political protests, her family was forced to flee abroad for four years. When they came

FIGURE 11 *Clémence Royer.* Les Hommes d'Aujourd'Hui, *1881.*

back to France, she had only a patchy education, but managed to qualify as a teacher. In her twenties, she decided to change her life. Bravely, she emigrated to Switzerland, where she started studying science and philosophy by herself in the local library.

Royer's new career began in 1859, the same year that Darwin's *Origin of Species* appeared in England. She embarked on several activities at the same time. She lectured to women about science, encouraging them not only to learn science, but also to change it. In addition, she wrote articles on politics and economics, won a prize for a book on income tax and fell in love. Controversially, she never married her partner, but they had one son and lived together until he died.

As soon as she read *The Origin of Species*, Royer recognised its importance. Darwin gave permission for her to translate his book, but later objected to some of the words she chose. He was even more surprised by the long preface she included. Royer claimed that human beings were affecting the course of evolution in a negative way. She believed that keeping sickly children alive would eventually weaken the whole human race. She also criticised men who chose beautiful wives rather than intelligent ones, insisting that clever mothers would mean cleverer children. Her translation and her comments strongly influenced how French scientists thought about Darwin's theories.

Because of their political activities, Royer and her partner lived in Italy for several years, where Royer wrote and lectured about science and evolution. When she returned to France, she became the first woman to be elected into a French scientific society – Paris's Anthropological Society. Many members were horrified, but she joined in the debates on evolution and published articles in their journal.

Royer said that she hated being trapped inside a woman's body. As an active feminist, she campaigned against scientists who agreed with Darwin that women are intellectually inferior to men. 'Up until now,' she wrote in 1874, 'science like law, made exclusively by men, has too often considered woman as an absolutely passive being.' Royer refused to believe that women were passive, and she thought that scientists were wrong to say so. Royer wanted women to succeed, and she wanted science to give them full credit for their abilities.

An Expert Amateur

Agnes Clerke (1842–1907) grew up in a small Irish village far away from any good schools, so she was educated by her parents. She never even went to university, yet she was one of Victorian Britain's most important astronomers because she wrote many books. Books are essential for the progress of science – without them, students and scientists can not learn about the latest research.

Astronomical knowledge exploded during Clerke's lifetime. Telescopes were getting bigger and better, and new techniques such as photography were being introduced. Throughout her childhood, Clerke devoured books, especially ones on astronomy. She first looked at the stars through her father's telescope in their back garden. He taught her how to tell the time from the stars so that they could set the village clocks – there was no radio or telephone to use.

When Clerke was 35, the whole family moved to London and she decided to become a scientific author. Her output was stunning: she wrote six large books, as well as hundreds of essays and articles. At first she wrote simple astronomy books for non-scientific readers, but later on she started writing for specialists. As well as describing the very latest discoveries, she suggested further questions that needed to be answered.

Clerke was both traditional and revolutionary. Like many other women, she wrote books for non-professional readers in which she stressed the religious importance of astronomy. Like generations of astronomers before her, she believed that the splendour of the night skies demonstrated that a magnificent God must have created the universe.

On the other hand, she invaded men's territory by discussing recent research and daring to point out problem areas. Many astronomers admired her enormously and valued her work. She was invited to carry out research at an observatory in South Africa, and an American scientist commented that 'there are very few living men who have her philosophical grasp of the whole subject and very few of equal erudition'. However, conservative scientists felt that women should not try to be scholars. One hostile critic exclaimed that 'the intuitive instinct of a woman is a safer guide to follow than her reasoning faculties'. Clerke was famous all over the world for her expertise, yet she was still excluded from professional science.

An American Astronomer

Maria Mitchell (1818–89) never studied at university, yet she dedicated herself to educating other women. She thought it was ridiculous to claim that women were no good at science. On the contrary, she argued, women made better astronomers than men because they had been trained to be more perceptive. For example, she claimed, doing fine needlework taught women how to judge small distances and to adjust delicate instruments.

Mitchell later wrote that her childhood helped her fall in love with astronomy. Her father was an amateur astronomer, her mother worked in two libraries so that she would have twice as many books to read, and she grew up in Nantucket, a part of America so flat and monotonous that it made the stars seem more attractive. Mitchell left school at sixteen, but studied books on advanced mathematics by herself at home.

For many years Mitchell ran a school library, but she practised astronomy in her spare time, and when she was 29 she discovered a new comet. From then on, her life was very different: unlike Agnes Clerke, she lived in America, where attitudes towards women were less repressive than in Britain. Mitchell was elected to two American Scientific Societies – and in both she was the first woman member. She started work as a human computer (mathematical calculator) for the US Navy. And when she was 44, she was invited to become the professor of astronomy at Vassar, a new all-female college which was completely independent of any other university.

Mitchell ran the observatory at Vassar for over twenty years. Instead of giving lectures, she preferred to teach her students in small groups and encourage them to get hands-on experience. She recognised that science involves creative thinking as well as methodical observation. She wrote: 'we especially need imagination in science. It is not all mathematics, nor all logic, but is somewhat beauty and poetry.' Since she constantly felt hampered by not having good instruments, she preferred to speculate about how data could be interpreted. Is Jupiter composed entirely of moving clouds? Are there invisible bodies in the universe that explain irregular orbits? Are the rings of Saturn different from the planet itself? These were some of the questions she pondered.

Several universities gave Mitchell honorary degrees, but she campaigned to raise money for more female colleges. Against much opposition, she argued what now seems obvious: it is unfair to compare men and women's scientific achievements because men benefited from a far better education.

The Fossil Collector of Lyme Regis

She sells sea shells on the sea shore
The shells that she sells are sea shells, I'm sure.

When people stumble over this tricky tongue-twister, they rarely realise that it was invented to describe **Mary Anning** (1799–1847), England's most famous fossil collector in the early 19th century. There are many romantic legends about her discoveries, yet Anning herself has disappeared behind them as though she were a mythical character rather than a real-life person.

There is very little firm evidence about Anning. For one thing, although her discoveries revolutionised geology, she never published anything herself. For most Victorians she was unimportant because she suffered from several disadvantages – she was a woman, she was poor and she lived in the countryside. Instead of finding out the truth about her, many writers preferred to write exciting stories, so that now it is difficult to sift out fact from fiction.

Anning's father was a carpenter who settled in a small English seaside town, Lyme Regis. He died when she was eleven, but before then he had taught his family how to scour the local cliffs at low tide and find fossils for tourists to buy. The fossils had to be rescued just after they had fallen from the cliff face, but before they were crushed by the incoming tide. This made collecting very dangerous, since another piece of rock could fall down at any moment. The Annings were willing to risk their lives because they were desperately short of money. So when Mary's elder brother Joseph found a large set of bones looking like a fish-cum-lizard, the whole family was very excited – especially when later on Mary Anning herself discovered the rest of the skeleton.

The Annings sold the fossil to a collector, who passed it on (at a profit, naturally) to a museum in London. Over the next few years, they found and sold several similar examples. These fossils, which later were called ichthyosaurs, aroused enormous interest among geologists because they could not be identified and did not match the skeletons of any known living animal. At that time many people believed that God had created the earth and all its creatures in 4004 BC (at 9 am on Monday 23 October, to be precise). Charles Darwin had not yet introduced his theory of evolution, and the word 'dinosaur' had not even been invented. Anning's fossils convinced geologists that the earth's animals used to be very different from those living now.

During the next few years, the Anning family gradually built up their fossil-selling business, but it was a precarious way to earn a living because sometimes long periods went by without finding a good fossil. When Mary Anning was around twenty, they were just about to sell the furniture to pay their rent. But a protector arrived – Thomas Birch, a wealthy collector who felt so sorry for them that he decided to help by auctioning off his own fossils. Purchasers arrived from all over Europe and the sale gave the Annings a huge amount of publicity, as well as some very welcome money.

Gradually Mary Anning took over the family business. She continued to sell fossils, and discovered several more that were entirely new. Geologists were baffled when she produced an animal nine feet long with a tiny head. An English geologist wrote in amazement: 'To the head of a Lizard, it united the teeth of a Crocodile; a neck of enormous length, resembling the body of a Serpent … the ribs of a Chameleon, and the paddles of a Whale.' A French anatomist dismissed the skeleton as a forgery, but when it was proved to be genuine, science had acquired a new creature – the plesiosaur – and also a new celebrity. Now geologists travelled to Lyme Regis to visit Mary Anning as well as to search for fossils. One artist showed her standing by the sea shore, holding the geological hammer she used for carefully picking out her fossils from the rocks (Figure 12, page 124).

Anning made several other major finds, but one of them in particular fascinated ordinary people, not just scientists – the flying reptile now called a pterodactyl, the first of these fossils to be found in Britain. With teeth like a crocodile, the body of a lizard and the wings of a bat, it seemed more like a dragon than an actual animal, and she became known as St Georgina of Lyme Regis, as if she had slain a mythical beast herself. Scientists argued long and bitterly about how ptero-dactyls should be classified, and Anning's exciting dis-coveries helped to make geology an even more popular science than it had been before.

Anning's pterodactyl is still owned by London's Natural History Museum, but although her fossils

FIGURE 12 *Mary Anning. Painting by William Gray, 1942.*

ended up in museums all over the world, her name has disappeared from many of them. Collectors in Lyme Regis bought her finds, and then sold (or sometimes gave) them to museums without insisting that her name be recorded. Anning's discoveries were vitally important for the growing science of geology, yet the credit went to the rich gentlemen who bought and analysed them. Many students have learnt about fossils by examining her discoveries, but remain ignorant of her name. 'The world has used me unkindly,' she wrote; 'I fear it has made me suspicious of all mankind'.

Visitors to Lyme Regis held different opinions about Mary Anning because she was earning her living in such an unconventional way. One geologist sneered that she was 'a prim, pedantic, vinegar looking, thin female', but another man was delighted to meet 'a strong, energetic spinster of about 28 years of age, tanned and masculine in expression'. In other words, she was behaving like a man – and many people found that hard to cope with.

Some men resented her intrusion into the male world of science, and scoffed at her Dorsetshire accent and her scanty education. But at least one wealthy woman was enormously impressed by her expertise. She explained how Anning had taught herself to identify bones and classify them scientifically, so that she was used to 'writing and talking with professors and other clever men on the subject, and they all acknowledge that she understands more of the science than anyone else in the kingdom'. Perhaps this rich visitor from London envied Anning, despite her poverty.

International Adventurers

A woman, let her be as good as she may, has got to put up with the life her husband makes for her.

George Eliot, *Middlemarch*, 1871–2

BEFORE YOU READ any further, name some famous explorers …

… think … think … think …

You probably suggested people who climbed to the top of mountains or landed on the moon – and all of them were probably men. Exploration is seen as a masculine activity: it's about being the first person to find the highest mountain or the longest river, and then mark it with a national flag. But even in the 19th century, women were travelling to unknown areas and writing very different sorts of stories about the world.

One way women found more freedom was by emigrating with their families to set up a new life away from industrial Britain. During the 19th century, women who travelled to distant parts of the world often led uncomfortable lives but had the advantage of being scientific pioneers. Before large towns and railways developed, they lived in isolated places far from shops and doctors. Women were responsible not only for organising food and meals, but also for looking after the family's health by treating them with herbs. This meant that women were the traditional experts in flowers and plants, and there was no firm boundary between this practical knowledge and the science of botany.

Catherine Traill explored the Canadian backwoods, and wrote several books describing plants and animals that Europeans had never encountered before. In Australia, **Louisa Meredith** also wrote detailed and beautiful biological accounts. However, like many Victorians, she held views about race which now seem repugnant, and it is easy to feel repelled by her descriptions of the local people she met.

Other female explorers came back to England to report on their experiences. Mary Kingsley went out to Africa with no interest in conquering either the continent or the people. Instead, she spent her time wading through swamps as she searched for rare fish and insects. In her books and lectures, she deliberately mocked herself as an eccentric woman who was both inside and outside her own English society. By doing this, she hoped that her audience would think carefully about what it meant for a European anthropologist to comment on African people.

Marianne North was another unconventional Victorian explorer. She travelled by herself all over the world. Her paintings enabled stay-at-home scientists – such as her friend Charles Darwin – to see distant scenes for themselves. Unlike professional botanists, she painted flowers as they grow naturally in the wild.

She built a special art gallery in Kew Gardens, and covered the walls with her lurid images of exotic plants. So if you visit London, you can see her vivid paintings exactly as she left them.

A Canadian Explorer

Until she was 30, **Catherine Traill** (1802–99) was a conventional English woman. Brought up in the countryside, she earned money by writing and spent her free time collecting flowers and reading books – science and geography as well as novels. But then her life changed dramatically: she emigrated to Canada with her Scottish husband.

In the 1830s much of Canada was still unexplored. There were hardly any universities, and scientists were more interested in practical subjects such as agriculture and mining than in theoretical research. Traill is important because she pioneered investigations into Canada's natural history and, through her writing, opened Canada up for English readers.

She had only been there for four years when she wrote her first book, *The Backwoods of Canada.* For the benefit of English people who were wondering whether or not to emigrate, she described her own experiences as an early settler. She pointed out the drawbacks as well as the delights. No nearby shops, neighbours or schools – yet on the other hand, there were new birds, plants and animals to enjoy. And for a woman, there was the unfamiliar freedom of being able to roam

128

through the forests and make scientific discoveries at first-hand rather than from books.

Traill had been pampered as a child, yet she thrived on the hard exciting life. Her husband, on the other hand, was unable to cope and relied on her. To support their large family – she gave birth to nine children – Traill wrote more and more books. As well as scouring the few works on natural history she could find, she made detailed observations and also asked the indigenous people (native American Indians) for information about plants and animals. Because she lived far away from any town, she was especially interested in local knowledge about herbs to use as medicines.

After Traill had been in Canada for a few years, she became very skilled at recognising and classifying flowers, and she built up a large collection of dried plants (a herbarium). She also came to learn the rhythm of the seasons, and to know which kinds of plants, birds and animals would be found together. An early ecologist, Traill protested about the way in which European immigrants were destroying the natural environment as they built large cities, factories and railways.

In her late fifties, Traill's life changed again. Her husband died, and like many other widows, she was forced to fend for herself. By this time, she was earning money from her books and she also – most unusually – managed to get a grant from England for her work. Canada itself was also altering. There were more universities and better roads, so that it was easier for her to travel to meet other botanists. Traill published two important books on Canadian wild flowers. Although she did include scientific terms, she wrote in a lively descriptive style because she wanted ordinary people to identify plants, and learn how they could be used for medicine, cooking and dyeing clothes.

Traill went on writing well into her nineties, but by then botany had become a professional science carried out in laboratories with expensive equipment. Some men accused her of being 'a struggling amateur' or 'a splendid anachronism'. However, other scientists admired her close detailed knowledge. Instead of automatically relying on European experts, Traill was an independent thinker who drew on her own specialised experience to lay the foundations of Canadian botany.

In the Australian Outback

Just as Catherine Traill made Canada familiar to English people, **Louisa Meredith** (1912–95) told them about life in Australia, a continent that seemed even stranger and further away – several months by boat.

Meredith was 27 when she set sail with her husband, and had already written books about English flowers. She was a good artist, and enjoyed gathering plants from obscure places so that she could paint them for her books. Mocking herself, she described the astonishment of some passers-by who saw her scrambling for a piece of gorse like 'a most uncouth young person'.

But out in the Australian bush, there was nobody watching and waiting to criticise her behaviour. English women were praised for being hardy travellers, and settlers like Meredith specialised in providing detailed descriptions of the environment. Meredith carefully labelled her pictures with the correct botanical terms, but she used poetical language to describe what she saw.

As a woman, she was expected to provide books that were a delight to read. This is one of her sentences from a long section on frogs: 'A vivid yellow-green seems the groundwork of the creature's array, and this is daintily pencilled over with other shades, emerald, olive, and blue greens, with a few delicate markings of bright yellow, like an embroidery in threads of gold on shaded velvet.' Dainty pencilling, gold embroidery – this was feminine writing very different from that of a male biologist. But Meredith made sure that her books were also informative and accurate so that they could be used by professional scientists.

Like many of her readers, Meredith found it impossible to be impartial about the indigenous people that she met. England's most famous Victorian scientist, Charles Darwin, believed not only that women were inferior to men, but also that the Australian aboriginals were inferior to Europeans. After the native Tasmanians were almost completely eliminated by white settlers, Meredith told tales of horror to confirm what English people wanted to hear – that the aboriginals deserved to die because they behaved so violently, almost like animals. Although she had described frogs and plants so meticulously and sympathetically, she declared that Tasmanians 'bore a curiously close resemblance to pug-dogs'.

Meredith's work might seem more like prejudiced travel stories than textbooks, but her writing was based on the theories scientists believed in at the time. Like modern TV programmes, her books taught ordinary people about foreign countries and the latest scientific ideas – but some of them now seem horribly wrong.

Suffering for Equality:
Universal Suffrage
and Universities

Suffering for Equality: Universal Suffrage and Universities

We are here to claim our right as women, not only to be free, but to fight for freedom. That is our right as well as our duty.

Christabel Pankhurst, *Votes for Women*, 1911

DURING THE SECOND half of the 19th century, women continued the fight for equality that had been launched by Mary Wollstonecraft at the end of the Enlightenment. In *A Vindication of the Rights of Woman*, she had explained, 'Some women govern their husbands, because intellect will always govern'. But although many wives probably did control their men, women campaigned fiercely for their independence to be legally recognised. In politics, they demanded universal suffrage – that women and men should all have the same right to vote. In education, women were claiming another right – to be able to study at university and compete in the same examinations as men.

Women set up protest movements all over the world, although some were more successful than others. The first country to give women the vote was New Zealand, in 1893, but the British campaigners were particularly renowned for their aggressive tactics. The most famous of these suffragettes was their leader, Emmeline Pankhurst, who accused the government of caring more about property than human life. As women chained themselves to railings and damaged wealthy homes, Pankhurst encouraged her followers by assuring them that 'The argument of the broken window pane is the most valuable argument in modern politics'.

Many suffragettes were sent to prison for their violent behaviour, but when the First World War broke out in 1914, they stopped their political activism and devoted themselves to patriotic work, often taking over jobs normally carried out by men. Having demonstrated their capabilities so clearly, at the end of the war women over 30 were granted the vote – although another ten years went by before women could vote at 21, the same age as men.

At the same time as this political activism, women were also fighting for the right to enter university. In 1865, Zurich became the first European university to admit women, and in England the first women's colleges were founded at Oxford and Cambridge in the 1870s. Nevertheless, Cambridge academics were so reactionary that it was not until 1948 that female graduates were allowed to claim their degrees, however brilliantly they performed in their examinations.

Many people – women as well as men – strongly opposed equal education. Some critics followed Darwin's line, arguing that God had deliberately designed the two sexes differently to make them suitable for different sorts of work. They insisted that if girls were educated they would not be good mothers, and maintained that their weak bodies would suffer if they used their brains too much. Selfish husbands worried that women might stop cooking meals and doing the housework. Even people in favour of teaching girls thought that men should be in charge of schools and universities. At a German meeting held in 1872 to discuss female education, the male delegates ate caviar and eels, while the women were served bread and butter in a separate room!

Medical Movements

*They cannot choose but to be women; cannot rebel success-
fully against the tyranny of their organisation ... if the
attempt to do so be seriously and persistently made, the
result may be a monstrosity – something which having
ceased to be woman is not yet man.*

Henry Maudsley, *Fortnightly Review,* 1874

T HE STRUGGLES IN medicine were particularly
bitter. For centuries, women had played vital roles
in caring for sick people, but the profession was very
hierarchical. Sex and class were both important. Most
obviously, men were doctors, while women were nurses
and midwives. But even the men used to be divided into
three ranks: physicians at the top, then surgeons and
finally, apothecaries (who made medicines, but were
less qualified than physicians and came from a lower
social class).

Breaking this long-established order seemed
unthinkable: men were horrified in the 19th century
when women dared to declare their intention of
becoming doctors. A Spanish student was stoned in
1881 when she turned up at medical school, and a
French class burnt a model of one courageous woman.

138

In Russia, people were slightly more tolerant because the country was desperately short of doctors; however, conditions must have been hard because out of the first group of 90 female medical students, 12 died before they could qualify. And in Britain, **Miranda Stuart** decided that the only way to overcome the official restrictions was to dress in disguise: she became a high-ranking army doctor by converting herself into James Barry, whose real sex was only revealed after she died.

When Sophia Jex-Blake was told that it was improper for a woman to attend medical lectures alone, she got around the ban by organising a group of women to study with her at Edinburgh. But when they went back for their second year, the male students threw mud at them and put a sheep in the classroom because, they explained, 'inferior animals' were being allowed in. Although Jex-Blake passed her exams, she was not allowed to register as a doctor. She managed to per-suade parliament to change the law, and she eventually qualified as a doctor at the Irish College of Physicians, which was more progressive than those in England and Scotland.

These battles were about power and prestige, not ability. It was women, not men, who were the traditional experts, especially in remote country areas where people had to fend for themselves. Women published self-help books for housewives that included recipes for brewing medicines and techniques for diagnosing ill-nesses. Some female herbalists specialised in particular remedies, which they sold throughout the country. In the English Midlands, Mrs Hutton experimented during the 18th century to find an effective treatment for heart problems with different potions made from foxgloves. She sold her secret recipe to Dr William Withering – and no prizes for guessing which of them became famous for discovering the drug with a Latin name, digitalis (the Latin botanical name for foxglove).

We know very little about the thousands and thousands of women who nursed sick people in the past. One pioneer for whom information has survived is Mary Seacole, who came from Jamaica. As a black woman, Seacole was doubly disadvantaged. Although she had extensive knowledge of European medicine as well as of traditional remedies, she could not train as a doctor because she was a woman, and she was refused employment as a nurse because she was black. During the Crimean War of 1853–6, Seacole funded her own trip to the battle zone, where she set up a hostel for sick officers and tended soldiers who had been wounded in action. One of her patients wrote that 'all the men swore by her, and in case of any malady, would seek her advice and use her herbal medicines in preference to reporting themselves to their own doctors'.

It was only in the 19th century that nurses started to be professionally trained. The world's first nursing school was founded in London by **Florence Nightingale**. Like Seacole, Nightingale became very famous in England for looking after injured soldiers during the Crimean War, but she benefited by coming from a far more privileged background. Since then, one of the few nurses to become famous is **Edith Cavell**, who sacrificed her own life to help soldiers escape during the First World War.

Other women were determined to reach the top of the medical profession and become doctors. When **Elizabeth Blackwell** wanted to train as a doctor in America, a lecturer (male, of course) suggested that she should attend his classes dressed as a man. Although she refused, there were probably several cross-dressing women who were never found out. Medical men invented cunning tactics to prevent women from invading their territory. When Blackwell came to England from America, the British Medical Association suddenly decided not to recognise American qualifications. **Elizabeth Garrett Anderson**, the first woman English doctor, sidestepped the regulations by taking the Apothecaries' examination – but the rules were immediately changed to stop that happening again.

These first female doctors strove to make sure that other women would find training easier, and they slowly gained ground. By the beginning of the First World War, Great Britain had almost five hundred female doctors, although these still came overwhelmingly from rich families. Unfortunately, legal equality is not the same as equality of opportunity. My own mother wanted to train as a doctor, but she had to become a nurse instead. Although she had come top in all her exams, my grandfather worked in a car factory and could not afford to send her to medical school.

Changing Identities

Miranda Stuart (1795–1865) was an orphan who was forced to fend for herself, although she did receive some secret help from influential relatives. Since she wanted to become a doctor, she dressed up as a man and called herself James Barry so that she could study first at Edinburgh Medical School and later in London. Although she maintained her new identity for the rest of her life, she was very unhappy because she could never behave naturally.

Once she was fully qualified, she joined the Army, where she found it very hard to keep up her deception (Figure 13). Stuart wore stacked heels and wrapped herself in towels to make herself look bigger, but she was often teased for her small size and high voice. She felt lonely and isolated, and her closest companions were her poodle and her servant, John. Like many people who find themselves in vulnerable positions, she protected herself by behaving aggressively. As James Barry, she acquired the reputation of being very hot-tempered and flirting outrageously with beautiful women. She (as him) fought duels and was arrested several times by the military police.

As Stuart rose up through the ranks, she served in several different countries, including India, South Africa and the Crimea (where she met Florence Nightingale). Eventually she reached the highest possible level – Inspector General of all the army hospitals in Canada. Despite Barry's reputation for violence, Stuart

FIGURE 13 *A photograph of Miranda Stuart/James Barry in Jamaica, around 1860. She is stroking her dog, called Psyche, and standing next to her servant, John*

was a skilful doctor whose patients welcomed her gentle touch. She cured many people simply by insisting that the beds and wards be kept scrupulously clean and not too crowded. In Cape Town (South Africa), she prevented many deaths by tracing a poisonous source infecting the water supply. Stuart had no qualms about making improvements, and radically overhauled hospital management systems. Tact, however, was not her strong point, and she earned bitter enemies by denouncing the cruelty and negligence of other doctors.

Stuart's closest friends and servants may well have been aware of her disguise, but the truth only became public after she died, when officials saw her body. Some people refused to believe that a woman could have achieved so much, and rumours spread that James Barry really had been a man. We shall never be certain: all the official records have mysteriously disappeared.

The Lady of the Lamp

Florence Nightingale (1820–1910) is often called 'The Lady of the Lamp' because of the long nights she spent alone on wards in army hospitals comforting wounded soldiers. She became one of Victorian England's most famous heroines because she made nursing into a respectable career, and she also campaigned to improve the appallingly unhygienic conditions at the battle front.

Nightingale's well-to-do father gave her an excellent education. When she was sixteen, she heard God's voice informing her that she had a mission to fulfil, but it was only nine years later that she realised what that mission was – to help the sick. At that time, there was very little training for nurses, and they were often said to be drunk, dirty and disreputable.

Her big chance came when she was 34. The Crimean War had started, and with the help of influential friends, Nightingale was sent out to Turkey to take charge of the army nursing, even though she herself was not a trained nurse. When she arrived, she was horrified. There were rats and fleas all over the nurses' rooms, and their daily water allowance was only one pint each for washing as well as for drinking. The wards were even worse: they were so overcrowded and short of supplies that wounded men lay untreated on filthy straw mattresses in the corridors.

The hospital was in complete chaos, but Nightingale had brought food, clothes and money with her. She threw herself into her work, and decided to tackle the dirt immediately. As first steps, she ordered two hundred scrubbing brushes and arranged for the men's clothes to be laundered. These simple strategies of cleaning the wards and the patients dramatically reduced the death rate.

As well as touring the wards and improving the standard of nursing, Nightingale was also immersed in administrative work. Every day she had countless letters to write, not only reports to army chiefs but also letters of sympathy to dead soldiers' relatives back home.

News of Nightingale's reforms seeped back to

England, where she was well on the way to becoming a national heroine. Yet out in Turkey, not everyone was so enthusiastic. The doctors resented her for interfering, while the nurses felt that she was a snob who looked down on them and refused to recognise their capabilities.

Nightingale's glorious reputation as 'The Lady of the Lamp' rests on her activities for less than two years, since she returned to London after the war ended. Soon after she got back, she became an invalid. Although she was never diagnosed with any physical illness, she spent much of the last 50 years of her life lying on a couch. In spite of this, Nightingale achieved a huge amount. Or was it perhaps because she was detached from normal social life that she managed to do so much? Not being involved in day-to-day activities must have given her a good deal of extra time.

By drawing up a long and critical report on her Turkish experiences, Nightingale helped to reform army nursing. She persuaded people to contribute money so that she could found the Nightingale School for Nurses at a London hospital, the first of its kind in the world.

In addition, Nightingale introduced new ways of compiling statistics to demonstrate the effectiveness of her methods. She was an intelligent, well-educated woman who had been denied the opportunity of going to university, yet she had enjoyed learning mathematics as a child. During the Crimean War, she devised special diagrams to make it immediately obvious that improving hygiene drastically cut the death rate. Back in England, she developed an official form to make it easier for hospitals to keep statistical data, and she even became a Fellow of the Royal Statistical Society. So perhaps she should be remembered not only as 'The Lady of the Lamp' but also as 'The Lady of the Ledger'.

A Nursing Martyr

Nursing is hard, dirty and emotionally exhausting work, but Florence Nightingale gave the profession a very positive image. Nurses were seen as saintly figures, as ministering angels who were paragons of self-sacrifice and devotion to duty. **Edith Cavell** (1865–1915) tried hard to match this stereotype, but she found that her dedication to saving lives came into conflict with the rules of warfare. Because of the decisions she made, she ended up in front of an army firing-squad, and after the First World War she rapidly became glorified as a heroic martyr.

The pay is small,
The food is bad,
I wonder why
I don't go mad.

This rhyme was not written by Cavell, even though it does describe the conditions she worked under as a nurse. Instead, the complaint was directed at Cavell's father, a country vicar, and was pencilled on the wall of

147

an attic room by one of the family's underfed and over-worked maids. Right through her childhood, Cavell was taught to live frugally and give charity to others: it seems her father did not realise that charity might start at home, with his own servants. He sent his daughter away to boarding schools where life was also hard. One pupil complained about the 'fearsome dragon' of a headmistress and the pervasive smell of 'cats, margarine and treacle'.

Cavell started work as a governess, but then decided to become a nurse. By the time that the First World War started in 1914, she had become head of a training school for nurses in Belgium, which was occupied by the German army, Britain's enemy. Cavell converted her hospital into a Red Cross clinic, and insisted on treating soldiers of every nationality – including Germans.

Soon she faced a moral dilemma. Her clinic became the centre of an underground organisation for helping British soldiers to escape into nearby Holland, which was neutral. Should she cooperate in saving their lives, or should she refuse to let her special Red Cross status be used in this way? She decided to break the rules and rescue the soldiers.

After a year, a spy informed on her, and Cavell was arrested along with two other members of the escape route team. And now she had another dilemma. She could declare that all three of them were innocent, but that would be lying, which in her eyes was a dreadful sin. On the other hand, if she told the truth, then she

148

would be incriminating her friends as well as herself. According to Cavell, the Germans themselves lied by telling her that her friends had confessed. Being an honest person herself, she believed them and revealed the group's illegal activities. As a consequence, all three of them were condemned to death.

Ten weeks later, Cavell was placed in front of a firing squad. Apparently one of the German soldiers threw down his gun and was himself killed for refusing to shoot her. After the war was over, Cavell's body was brought back to England for two burial services, one in Westminster Abbey and the other near her childhood home. From the German perspective, executing Cavell had been a foolish decision, because British propaganda campaigns influenced world opinion by denouncing the Germans as murderous monsters who had slain a helpless heroine.

America's First Doctor

Although **Elizabeth Blackwell** (1821–1910) was born in England, when she was eleven her parents emigrated to America. She decided to become a doctor because she wanted to fight against inequality. Seventeen medical schools rejected her application, but according to the stories (which may or may not be true) Geneva College, in New York state, accepted her by mistake: the students had voted to accept her as a joke, and were astonished when she turned up for classes.

While she was training, Blackwell had to put up with

people staring at her as if she were a strange animal or perhaps completely mad. The lecturers asked her not to attend the classes on sex and reproduction – but she did, because she was set on becoming fully qualified. To improve her education, Blackwell went to study in Paris, but found that she could only train as a midwife. Then she tried London, but was not allowed to practice as a doctor. When she went back to America, she complained that she faced 'a blank wall of social and professional antagonism' – the other doctors resented her, the patients didn't trust her and everybody thought she was strange.

Blackwell was forced to be realistic. She knew that however skilled she was as a doctor, she was never going to achieve the same status as her male colleagues. She opened a hospital for very poor people, and gave other women the opportunity to train there. She believed that women should receive the same education as men, but was forced to accept that women-only colleges were better than none. In 1868, she founded a Women's Medical College in New York, but the next year, left her sister to run it while she went back to England.

While she was in England, Blackwell campaigned to improve conditions for female doctors. Many illnesses were caused by dirt, and she led the way in using antiseptics and stressing the importance of hygiene. Being the first woman doctor is a splendid achievement, but Blackwell is just as important because she fought for good health for everyone, not only the rich.

When she qualified as a doctor, an American

journalist commented: 'as this is the first case of the kind that has been perpetrated either in Europe or America, I hope, for the honor of humanity, that it will be the last'. As a pioneer, Blackwell was often insulted, but she was determined to prove that this critic was wrong – by encouraging younger students, she made sure that she was not the last woman doctor.

A Medical Suffragette

Elizabeth Garrett Anderson (1836–1917) was a committed feminist, and – unlike most of the women in this book – insisted on keeping her maiden name (Garrett) after she married James Anderson. Her father was a pawnbroker who became rich and wanted his daughters to be well-educated ladies of leisure. But after engineering a meeting with Elizabeth Blackwell, Garrett Anderson decided that there was only one thing she wanted to do – become a doctor. Even though Blackwell's example made Garrett Anderson's life slightly easier, she found that the medical world was still extremely prejudiced against women. She also had to overcome the objections of her parents, who insisted that she get married like her friends.

Eventually she won them round. No medical school would accept her, so she trained as a nurse but attended the medical lectures. The other students (all male) asked for her to be banned. Why? Because she embarrassed them by being top of the class. Hospital doctors protested that 'the presence of a young female

151

in the operating theatre is an outrage to our natural instincts and is calculated to destroy the respect and admiration with which the opposite sex is regarded'.

With her father's financial backing, Garrett Anderson set up a medical practice in London. She still wanted to go to university, but could only find a place in Paris. After making a special study of migraine, in 1870 she became France's first woman doctor. But of course, when she got back the English profession refused to recognise her French degree!

Garrett Anderson founded clinics and hospitals to treat women patients, and employed women to run them. But for nineteen lonely years Anderson was the only female member of the British Medical Association. At the same time as reforming medicine, Garrett Anderson was campaigning for equality and the right to vote. After the laws discriminating against women had relaxed, she became England's first female mayor. Through her political work in the suffragette movement, Garrett Anderson helped to improve women's education as well as their health.

Women and Universities

If women were to control the government, the state would be in danger, for they do not act according to the dictates of universality, but are influenced by accidental inclinations and opinions. The education of women goes on one hardly knows how.

Georg Wilhelm Friedrich Hegel, *The Philosophy of Right,* 1821

WOMEN CAMPAIGNED FOR better education throughout the 19th century, but attitudes changed extremely slowly. There were several problems to overcome before it became possible for girls to have the same opportunities for university education as boys. One of them was practical: girls needed to be better taught at school if they were going to study at university later. At the end of the Enlightenment, some women – including Charles Darwin's aunts – set up schools where girls could learn science, but the situation only improved gradually.

Many parents remained adamantly opposed to educating girls. Daughters had to fight not only against prejudiced fathers, but also against mothers who thought that girls belonged at home to help them with the housework. Some daughters organised pressure groups to make their families change their minds. In 1901, a fifteen-year-old German girl called Karen described how 'Three of Mother's friends came one after the other yesterday, to work on Mother to send me to the High School. Mother spoke with Father afterwards'. She also recruited her brother and her aunt to 'work on him too'. After her father finally relented, Karen wrote: 'Oh how happy I am! And thankful!!'

But after she had successfully completed her school education, Karen was faced with a dilemma. Should she go on to university, or should she marry her boyfriend? Most people believed that it was impossible for a woman to have a good career and also be a good wife and mother – well into the 20th century, many women had to resign from their jobs when they got married. Even Karen felt that she had to choose between university and marriage. Luckily for science, she opted for education rather than romance, and later became the famous psychoanalyst Karen Horney.

By the 1870s, everybody agreed that some education for women was essential, even if only to make them more interesting partners for their husbands, and better mothers for teaching their sons how to read and write. However, most people thought that girls should be educated differently from boys, since they would be leading different lives in the future.

Life was very hard for the first women teachers, who inherited the social slurs that had been cast at governesses (as in *Jane Eyre*). Critics sneered that they were not real women, because they could never love a husband or have children of their own. That's the point of this cruel rhyme about Dorothea Beale and Frances Buss, two famous 19th-century campaigners for girls' schools in England:

Miss Buss and Miss Beale
Cupid's darts do not feel
How different from us,
Miss Beale and Miss Buss.

In Britain, the leading activist for female education was Emily Davies. She insisted that girls would never get accepted at university until they could pass the same entrance examinations as boys. By the middle of the 19th century, enough girls had reached this standard to persuade colleges first at London (in 1848), and later at Cambridge (1869) and Oxford (1879) to take female students. At Cambridge, **Ida Freund**, a German chemist, became one of the earliest women lecturers. Other Cambridge science graduates introduced still further reforms, including **Hertha Ayrton**, who embarked on a scientific career and became the first woman to present her own research paper at London's Royal Society.

Education improved partly because some women struggled so that their daughters could have the careers they themselves had been denied. Although a few husbands were sympathetic to their wives' complaints, they explained that 'You must fight your own battles'. In America, **Elizabeth Agassiz**, a professor's wife, campaigned for women's science education and founded Radcliffe College in 1894. She had not been to university herself, but was determined that younger women should have better opportunities.

Progress was not always straightforward. In Russia, women were first allowed to enter universities in 1876. However, from 1881 to 1905 this right was taken away from them again, because the Czar had been assassinated by a woman. Like many of her clever friends, **Sofia Kovalevskaia** left Russia and went to a more liberal German university. She was a brilliant mathematician, but had been born too early and in the wrong country. Half a century later, **Grace Hopper** was able to study at America's top universities and to pursue the type of career that had – until very recently – been open only to men.

A Chemist at Cambridge

Men were very sceptical about admitting women to Cambridge. They divided female scientists into two imaginary stereotypes: delicate fragile creatures incapable of intellectual work, and muscular freaks who scarcely deserved to be called women. At the end of the 19th century, the first real-life female scholars struggled to show that they were normal women as well as being excellent scientists (Figure 14).

Ida Freund (1863–1914) spent her childhood in Austria, and was furious about being forced to leave her native country when her uncle decided that she should

FIGURE 14 *Teaching staff at Cambridge in 1896.*

study science at Cambridge, one of the earlier European universities to admit women. Despite speaking poor English and knowing very little mathematics, she managed to win first-class honours in her examinations. But that didn't mean she got her degree! However well they did in their finals, women at Oxford and Cambridge could not graduate formally until after the First World War.

Freund (third from the left on the front row of Figure 14) became an inspiring teacher who devoted her life to science education. Because women could not work in the same laboratories as men, she taught special classes in chemistry at Newnham College, Cambridge, which still only accepts girls. She also wrote text books, and organised holiday workshops for women teachers. She felt angry that physics was so badly taught in girls' schools, and raised money to buy better instruments.

Her students adored her. At first they were terrified when she told them off for making mistakes, but they soon realised that she wanted them to achieve the highest possible results. She joined in the jokes about her foreign accent, and provided cakes and chocolates before the exams.

However, Freund's appearance made her an easy target. She had lost one leg in a cycling accident and needed a wheelchair to get around. Spiteful critics focused on her looks, ignoring her brains and hard work. One scientist cruelly suggested that she should exercise more to lose weight.

It was difficult for Freund and the other female lecturers to know what to wear, because they were criticised whatever they chose. As this photograph shows,
some women wore shirts and ties, so they were accused
of being pseudo-men. But dressing in a feminine way
wasn't the solution either, because then other people
(women as well as men) could say that these female pioneers were more interested in fashion than in education.

The Royal Society's First Feminist

Hertha Ayrton (1854–1923) was one of the earliest students at Girton College in Cambridge. She had to
struggle so hard to establish a scientific career for herself that she became an ardent campaigner for women's
rights. She wanted to save female students who followed her from enduring the same bad experiences.

Like many women, Ayrton found examinations very
stressful, and despite her high ability, she repeatedly
under-performed. However, she decided to ignore
her poor results and embark on research. She married
her physics professor, but although she still did some
academic work she felt frustrated by being forced to
spend so much time looking after her children and her
husband. After ten years, she managed to get back to
her research into electricity, which was important for
electric arc lamps; later she switched to examining the
ripple patterns in sand. As well as publishing several
papers and a book on electricity, Ayrton invented

scientific instruments – including the Ayrton Flapper Fan, designed for soldiers to flap away poison gas during the First World War.

Ayrton's first paper at the Royal Society, on electricity, was presented by one of her husband's friends, but in 1904 she became the first woman to read her own paper to the Society – 'The Origin and Growth of Ripple Marks'. Although eight Fellows nominated her to join the Society, she was disqualified for a strange reason – she was married!

When some of her own work was attributed to her husband, Ayrton was furious, and she became increasingly active in the suffragette movement. She often denounced sexual discrimination in science, and her words are still relevant today: 'I do not agree with sex being brought into science at all. The idea of "woman and science" is completely irrelevant. Either a woman is a good scientist, or she is not; in any case she should be given opportunities, and her work should be studied from the scientific, not the sex, point of view.'

An American Campaigner

Elizabeth Agassiz (1822–1907) was born before women were able to go to university, but throughout her life she campaigned for young women to gain the scientific education that she would have loved to have had herself. She came from a wealthy Boston family, and her parents hired governesses to teach her languages, music and other subjects suitable for girls. Yet despite this conventional childhood, Agassiz made important contributions to science as well as to female education.

She chose an unusual husband – Louis Agassiz, a Swiss biologist who became a professor at Harvard University. He carried out important research into glaciers, fossils and fish, and she wrote excellent books that enabled many people to learn about his work. Their marriage became a scientific and business partnership in which the Swiss scientist depended on his American wife. She taught him English, organised his financial affairs, recorded observations during his scientific expeditions and edited his books. Like many other scientific couples, he took the credit for work which he could not have completed without her.

They made three long scientific expeditions together, to Brazil, Cuba and the South American coast. Although Elizabeth Agassiz had supposedly been a delicate child, she abandoned her elegant drawing-room clothes and went exploring in men's trousers and boots, which at that time was a shocking way for a lady to behave. She kept a daily journal, and became a skilled natural historian who took notes during her husband's lectures and helped him improve them. In other words, they worked as a team. She wrote home to her family that 'We lecture three times a week'. Her records formed the basis for their joint book about Brazil, and she also published her own book about zoology. On their nine-month sea-voyage, he devised a new theory about glaciers, but it was Elizabeth Agassiz who wrote the articles essential for communicating his ideas.

Scientific research was an expensive activity, and the Agassiz couple were always short of money. She took over all the administrative work of their scientific enterprise, charmed rich businessmen into donating money and ran a girls' school for eight years. After he died in 1873, she continued to popularise his work but also became very involved in female education. Along with other campaigners, Elizabeth Agassiz founded Radcliffe College as an annex to Harvard University. As Radcliffe's first President, Agassiz enabled many young women to study science at an advanced level, but it was not until 1943 that Harvard allowed women into its classrooms.

A Russian Mathematician

Sofia Kovalevskaia (1850–91) was a brilliant mathematician, whose life sounds like a romantic adventure story, even though she was often very unhappy. In 1888, she impressed the judges in a French competition so much that they increased the prize money, and she became a mathematics professor at Stockholm University. Rebellion was her recipe for success, but she was forced to fight against male chauvinists like the Swedish playwright August Strindberg, who called her 'a pernicious and unpleasant phenomenon – even, one might say, a monstrosity'.

Kovalevskaia was born in Russia but later she travelled all over Europe to get a good education and to work. Like her clever friends and sisters, she was determined to obtain a degree – and that meant going abroad, because Russian universities still excluded women. To own a passport, she had to be married, so she chose an eligible young student (Vladimir Kovalevskaia), even though she didn't love him. Together they travelled to Germany, where she eventually succeeded in getting permission to take some courses in maths and physics.

In Berlin, one maths professor strongly disapproved of women, so he gave her exceptionally hard problems to put her off. But his tactic failed, because she solved them successfully. From then on, he supported Kovalevskaia and made sure that she got her doctorate, even though she was not allowed to attend lectures and some examiners deliberately failed women.

Kovalevskaia was a highly qualified mathematician, but nobody would give her a job. In despair, she went back to Russia with Vladimir where she decided to abandon mathematics and enjoy herself. After a few years of expensive clothes and parties, the money ran out and her husband committed suicide. Afterwards, she managed to become a professor in Sweden, where there was more support for female equality.

Mathematically, this was a productive period in Kovalevskaia's life, when at last she won prizes, published papers and became known throughout Europe. She specialised in using mathematics to solve physical problems, such as the structure of Saturn's rings, the movement of light through crystals and the rotation of solid objects.

Mathematicians are often said to be unemotional and lack imagination. Kovalevskaia illustrates how faulty that stereotype can be. She soon got bored with Stockholm and longed to be in a big city like Paris or St Petersburg. She started writing plays and novels, some of which were very successful. And she fell in love. Like many women, she faced a hard decision. Should she move to Paris and marry the man she loved, or should she stay in Sweden and pursue her career? But before she could make up her mind, she died of pneumonia in the hard Stockholm winter after dutifully returning to give some lectures.

A Naval Programmer

When she was a child, **Grace Hopper** (1906–92) loved taking alarm clocks to bits to see how they worked. Instead of getting angry, both her parents encouraged her to enter what was then the male world of maths and engineering. Her mathematical mother had been born too early to be a pioneer, but Hopper was determined to ignore discrimination against women. She succeeded in one of the most difficult careers she could have chosen, although she later said that she would have become a civil engineer if it had been possible.

Hopper was educated at two of America's top universities. She was a student at Vassar, an all-girls College founded in 1861, and she got her doctorate from Yale. She taught mathematics at Vassar for twelve years, but she changed direction when the Second World War started. Hopper wanted passionately to serve her country by joining the Navy, but all sorts of official objections were raised to this extremely unusual request – she was too old, she didn't weigh enough, women were better at teaching than fighting, and so on. But Hopper was good at fighting. She argued her way into the Navy, and went to work at Harvard University on Mark I, one of the world's earliest computers. The most famous photograph of Hopper shows her proudly wearing her naval uniform (Figure 15, page 166).

During the war Hopper developed computer programs to calculate angles for firing guns in different weather conditions. The first computers were enormous and very erratic. Hopper carefully preserved a moth that had made a computer break down by flying inside it – literally a bug in the system. Ten years later, she gave the word 'debug' its modern sense of removing programming mistakes.

Hopper was only 40 years old when the Navy declared that she had to retire, so she changed over to developing business computers. At that time, making a computer work was very difficult because virtually no software existed. All the instructions had to be written in complicated mathematical codes. Hopper transformed programming by inventing new languages which were more like ordinary English.

Before small personal computers and lap-tops were introduced, giant computers occupying several rooms were used commercially for doing accounts and working out salaries. This became Hopper's area of specialisation. In 1967, after the Navy's payroll program had repeatedly gone wrong, they changed their mind about

FIGURE 15 *Grace Hopper in naval uniform*

her age and begged her to come back and help sort out the problems. Hopper worked for the Navy until she was 80 years old, and was one of the first women to be promoted to the high rank of Rear Admiral.

Hopper's shining example encouraged other women

to make their careers in the computer industry. She received many prestigious medals, but she was especially honoured by the Data Processing Management Association in 1967, which chose her for its first 'Man-of the Year' award!

The Modern Era:
Exclusion and Exploration

The Modern Era: Exclusion and Exploration

I went off on holiday and came back to the lab wearing an engagement ring. That was the stupidest thing I ever did. In those days married women did not work.

Jocelyn Bell Burnell, 2004

BY THE MIDDLE of the 20th century, women were enjoying far more freedom than ever before. Although they were excluded from many private clubs, they could study at university and join scientific societies. Nevertheless, women still did not have the same opportunities as men, and from the 1960s onwards, feminists waged aggressive campaigns for equality. All over the world supporters of Women's Liberation Movements argued that even though women might be in a strong position legally, in practice they were being relegated to inferior, subordinated roles.

Science was one of the most obvious areas in which women were discriminated against. Scientific research was still overwhelmingly carried out by men, and female scientists complained bitterly about their treatment, gathering together evidence of how women were being excluded from top-level science. They protested that they were rarely promoted, were allocated unexciting research topics, were left out of laboratory discussion groups and were often paid less for doing the same work. Some female scientists are still voicing similar complaints.

Nobel Prizes

But if God had wanted us to think just with our wombs,
why did He give us a brain?

Clare Booth Luce, *Life*, 1970

PEOPLE WHO PROTEST about discrimination often point out how few women have won a Nobel Prize. The system was set up by Alfred Nobel, a Swedish millionaire who invented dynamite (strange that one of his prizes is for peace!). Starting in 1901, three science awards are made every year – in physics, chemistry, and physiology or medicine. Each winner receives some money, a diploma and a large gold medal (you can see its design in Figure 2 on page 24).

In principle, both men and women are eligible. In reality, the picture is different. During the entire 20th century, only five women received chemistry or physics prizes, compared with several hundred men. Even the medical prize has only been awarded to six women. The first woman to win a Nobel medal for science was **Marie Curie**. Almost 100 years later, by the time of the Nobel centenary celebrations in 2001, the only female prizewinner from Britain was the chemist **Dorothy Hodgkin**.

The Nobel Committee makes its decisions in secret, but suspicious delays and omissions suggest that some women may have been unfairly discriminated against. Because great scientific discoveries often depend on team work, the prizes can be distributed among up to three winners. There have been several instances of joint awards where many people feel that a woman deserved to share a Prize, but was excluded because of her sex; the most famous examples are **Lise Meitner** and **Rosalind Franklin**.

However, the situation is not always clear-cut, and there are usually arguments on both sides. Without a doubt, many women have not been given all the credit they deserve. But does that imply that all women have been dramatically underrated? Some critics accuse women of strengthening their case unfairly by relying on accusations of sexual discrimination.

Joyce Bell Burnell is a British astronomer who worked with the Cambridge team that discovered pulsars in the 1960s. She still complains bitterly about the laboratory atmosphere, and found it extremely difficult being the only woman. According to Burnell, she should have shared the Nobel Prize that was awarded to her supervisor. Nevertheless, her opponents maintain that it is quite normal for only the head of a large research group to be rewarded.

There are other controversial examples. Some historians claim that the Nobel prizewinner Albert Einstein may not have been working alone. Einstein is celebrated for being a genius with a super-human brain, but they suggest that he developed his ideas together with his wife, **Mileva Einstein**, who was also a physicist. Einstein was the most famous scientist of the 20th century, and even people who have no idea what his theories are about know that he introduced the theory of relativity and the equation $e = mc^2$. If his wife were his hidden collaborator, then a woman would have been responsible for the most fundamental theories of modern physics. Unsurprisingly, not everyone agrees that she played such a crucial role.

Martyr to Radioactivity

Only one person, man or woman, has ever won two Nobel Prizes – **Marie Curie** (1867–1934), the world's most famous female scientist, who died as a result of her research into radioactivity. In 1903, she shared the physics prize with her husband Pierre and the French scientist Henri Becquerel; in 1911, she received the chemistry prize on her own for discovering two new elements, radium and polonium.

Curie spent most of her life in Paris, but she chose the name polonium in honour of the country where she was born – Poland (her original name was Manya Sklodowska). Her family was very poor, and she worked as a governess to earn money so that her sister could study medicine in Paris. Eventually she managed to reach Paris herself, where she got two degrees, one in physics and one in mathematics. There were over 1,800 students in the Science Faculty, but only 23 women. Like many of her friends, Curie was often cold and hungry, but she was exuberant about being free to learn after years of struggle. 'It was like a new world opened to me,' she remembered, 'the world of science, which I was at last permitted to know in complete freedom.'

When she was 27 years old, she married Pierre, a quiet reclusive chemist. Although they soon had their first baby, Marie Curie was determined to go on working, and she chose a new and exciting topic – radioactivity. X-rays had just been discovered (in 1895) and they seemed like magic: for the first time, doctors could see the bones inside people's bodies. The following year, Becquerel discovered by accident that photographic plates are affected by uranium compounds as if they were emitting some sort of special light. Curie set out to solve the mystery.

First she searched for other substances with similar properties. She devised an electrical technique which demanded phenomenal precision. Colleagues described how she would sit for hours in an unheated room manipulating her apparatus as though she were sensitively playing a piano. After her first results seemed promising, Pierre Curie decided to help her. Within a few months, they had found their first new element, polonium. But although they did not realise it, they were already making themselves ill by working so closely with radioactive materials.

Their next discovery was even more important because it enabled Marie Curie to work out why some substances are radioactive. Uranium is extracted from a natural ore called pitchblende, and she showed that the more uranium there is in the pitchblende, the more radioactive it is. As she explained, 'My experiments proved that the radiation of uranium compounds … is an atomic property of the element of uranium.' At the time it was extraordinary to think that this effect was nothing to do with traditional chemistry, light or heat. It appeared as if Curie had uncovered a natural perpetual energy machine right inside the atom. Her ideas helped to overturn conventional physics, which believed that atoms were solid balls, nature's tiniest building blocks.

For the next three years, the Curies purified tons of pitchblende in order to obtain pure samples of radium and polonium. This was hard physical work, carried out in an old shed which was freezing in winter and suffocating in summer. Curie was so committed to research that she seemed almost to welcome this hardship, although she did say later that she was not sure they would have started if they had known what a minute fraction they were searching for. Purification involves tedious repetitive chemical processes which are extremely time-consuming, but Curie was also publishing theoretical papers. This was one of the most productive periods of her life, when she was helping to revolutionise physics. Yet she had no official job, no doctorate and very little money.

Eventually the Curies' dedication paid off – in 1899 they isolated pure radium, which emitted an eerie blue-green glow in the darkness. Marie Curie's own life also

FIGURE 16 *Marie Curie. Caricature of Pierre and Marie Curie by Julius Mendes Price,* Vanity Fair, *1904.*

started to glow, as she obtained industrial backing for her research. At last she could work in a proper laboratory, and was paid a salary. She soon became world-famous because radium was exciting not only for theoretical physicists, but also for doctors who advertised radium as a wonder treatment for cancer and skin complaints – in the early days, nobody realised how dangerous it is.

In 1903, the couple were awarded the Nobel Prize for their work on radioactivity, although many people regarded Marie Curie merely as her husband's assistant. This cartoon (Figure 16) shows Pierre Curie triumphantly holding up a shining crystal while she leans admiringly on his shoulder – he looks like the heroic discoverer, and she looks like his adoring little helper. He is even holding a book, whereas she had carried out much of the theoretical work. Pictures such as this helped to reinforce the wrong idea that women are incapable of independent scientific research.

In spite of her fatigue from radioactivity poisoning, Marie Curie's career blossomed, and she was deeply in love with Pierre. Together with their two daughters, Irène and Eve, they enjoyed long family holidays. Only three years later, disaster struck: Pierre was killed in a traffic accident. Marie Curie was devastated.

In an attempt to get over her grief, she threw herself into her work. She became France's first female professor, and also headed her own laboratory, which she made into a leading research centre by accumulating as much radium as possible. In her honour, a new physical unit called the Curie was invented to provide a way of measuring radioactivity. In 1911, she received her second Nobel Prize, this time for her isolation of radium and polonium (it is quite normal for Nobel Prizes to be awarded several years after the event they celebrate).

The First World War (1914–18) completely disrupted Marie Curie's research. She packed her precious radium in a large lead box, too heavy for her to carry, and took it to the south of France in case the Germans attacked Paris. Then she concentrated on organising an emergency X-ray service, including special ambulances called 'little Curies' which travelled to battlefields so that wounded soldiers could be treated immediately. Her radiological units carried out a million wartime examinations.

After the war, Marie Curie embarked on a publicity campaign to get more radium for research in physics and medicine. She travelled all over the world, and she campaigned for different countries to forget their political differences and cooperate scientifically. Her elder daughter, Irène, worked with her at the Radium Institute and – like her mother – she was awarded a Nobel Prize for her research into radioactivity. Irène had been brought up to believe that 'equality between man and woman is entirely natural', and she fought for women's rights.

Marie Curie suffered greatly from having worked so closely with radioactive materials. She could not conceal the radiation burns on her fingers, but she did try to ignore severe symptoms of the leukaemia that was killing her, and continued experimenting almost until the end of her life. She died deliriously whispering about radium. As she had requested, she was buried with her husband, and Polish soil was scattered over her coffin.

Although Marie Curie was world-famous, she was often ostracised by old-fashioned scientists. Many people refused to believe that a woman was capable of independent research and continued to portray her as her husband's humble helper. She was treated differently from men: her friendship with another scientist was blown up into a huge scandal that nearly cost her the Nobel Prize.

Since then, biographers – including her daughter Eve – have tried to restore Curie's reputation by emphasising her hard work. However, exaggerating her dedication can also be misleading. Some stories make Curie into an abnormal woman who never smiled, scarcely ate and selflessly sieved through pitchblende as though she were some sort of glorified scientific cook. She herself thought that her work and the research institutes she founded were more important than the fact that she was establishing a female first. Rather than being celebrated as an unusual woman, she wanted to be remembered as an outstanding scientist.

A Chemical Star

Over 50 years after Marie Curie, the British scientist **Dorothy Hodgkin** (1910–94) won the Nobel Prize for chemistry. She was nominated several times, but she did not receive her Prize until eight years after she discovered the structures of penicillin and Vitamin B12.

Hodgkin was trained as a chemist, and she spent her scientific life at Oxford and Cambridge. Her work had many medical applications because she specialised in analysing vitamins and hormones. She started her research in 1932, and during the Second World War she studied penicillin so that it could be produced artificially to cure injured soldiers. Hodgkin then solved a problem thought to be impossible: finding the structure of Vitamin B12, a complicated molecule that people need in their bodies to avoid becoming anaemic. After receiving her Nobel Prize, Hodgkin unravelled a third important compound – insulin, which is vital for treating diabetes.

Hodgkin had to overcome many difficulties to continue working at such a high level. She was in Ghana when she heard about her Nobel Prize, because her husband studied African history and they had two homes, one in England and one in Africa. Hodgkin was a very energetic woman who brought up three children as well as having an outstanding career. This combination of science and motherhood was far more unusual then than now. In addition, she suffered from painful arthritis in her hands, which made it exceptionally difficult for her to carry out delicate experiments.

Many of Hodgkin's male colleagues commented on her good looks, a compliment that annoys women who feel she should be congratulated on her brains rather

FIGURE 17 Dorothy Hodgkin. *Maggi Hambling, 1985.*

than her beauty. However, artists have found ways of focusing on her achievements rather than on her face. One of them, the famous sculptor Henry Moore, drew a picture of her hands, which were cruelly gnarled and twisted by arthritis; in this way, he paid tribute to her experimental skills. Her hands are also an important feature in another portrait (Figure 17, page 183). The artist has emphasised Hodgkin's scientific success by painting her with a large molecular model surrounded by piles of papers. But she also has a double set of hands, blurred to give the impression of how quickly this dynamic chemist moved from one task to another. Amid the work heaped up on her desk, there's even a half-eaten sandwich that she has been too busy to finish.

A Jewish Physicist

Lise Meitner (1878–1968) suffered from a double disadvantage – she was a woman, and she was Jewish. She went to university in Vienna, but after she got a doctorate in theoretical physics, she could only find work as a school teacher. She decided instead to go to Berlin and carry out research into radioactivity, but she was made to feel strange and unwelcome there. People were so astounded to see a woman physicist that when she gave a university lecture on 'Cosmic processes' the newspapers reported it as 'Cosmetic processes'. For seven years she worked in her laboratory without pay, but eventually she scored two firsts for a female scientist in Germany: she gained a salaried job, and then became a professor in 1919.

For 31 years Meitner carried out important experiments which helped to lay down the foundations for atomic physics. When she started in 1907, radioactivity had only recently been discovered, and scientists were very enthusiastic about this new source of power. Meitner examined many chemicals to find new radio-active elements and explain why they constantly emit energy. She often collaborated with the chemist Otto Hahn, and in the 1920s they moved together into the new field of nuclear physics. By now she was close friends with many of Germany's leading scientists, and was invited to international conferences as one of the world's leading experts.

When Adolf Hitler came to power, many Jewish scientists were forced to emigrate. Some Germans even denounced Albert Einstein's relativity as 'Jewish physics'. However, Meitner decided to stay in Berlin. She had converted to Christianity, and later said that the physics department she had built up there was 'my life's work, and it seemed so terribly hard to separate myself from it'. Together with Hahn, she started to investigate nuclear reactions.

By 1938, it was too dangerous for Meitner to live in Germany, and she left illegally with only a few clothes and virtually no money, eventually joining a research laboratory in Sweden. Although she felt miserable and isolated, she continued to write letters to Hahn discussing their work. When Hahn obtained some un-expected results, he turned to her for help. With her nephew Otto Frisch, Meitner solved Hahn's problem by working out how a uranium nucleus could split in two and release a gigantic amount of energy. This is the reaction that lies at the heart of the atomic bomb.

Their long, close collaboration came abruptly to an

end after Hahn published a paper separately from her, even though he had been helped by her insights. Working together, Meitner and Hahn had played a crucial role in modern physics, but although Meitner was nominated for a Nobel Prize, only Hahn received one. After the end of the Second World War, he scarcely mentioned her. Perhaps, she commented, he was trying to suppress his memories of having worked so closely with a non-Aryan woman.

Victim of Discrimination

If **Rosalind Franklin** (1920–58) had not died so young, then perhaps she would have won a Nobel Prize for her work on the double helix structure of DNA. In 1962, three men were awarded the prize for DNA, and many people feel that she was treated unfairly.

The story begins in 1942 when Franklin graduated from Cambridge and started investigating coal as her contribution to wartime scientific research. She became an expert in X-ray crystallography, a technique for working out the internal structure of a substance from patterns of dots and streaks on an X-ray photograph.

Because of her achievements she was invited to spend four years in a Paris laboratory, where her colleagues were impressed by her experimental skill and her single-minded dedication to her research. Franklin loved being in Paris: she made great progress in her work, had many friends and enjoyed walking holidays in the mountains. Unfortunately, unlike now, it was difficult for British people to work in Europe, so she accepted a job at King's College, London. And this was when her career started to go wrong.

In Paris Franklin had been treated as an equal, but in London she soon realised that women were discriminated against. She was even banned from entering the special coffee room where male scientists often discussed their work. In addition, her position was unclear. She had been told that she would be in charge of the X-ray diffraction unit, but in fact a senior researcher called Maurice Wilkins was already using X-rays to analyse DNA. From the very beginning, Franklin felt that she was excluded from normal laboratory life, and her relationship with Wilkins deteriorated until they were scarcely on speaking terms.

The situation became still more complicated when two scientists at Cambridge, James Watson and Francis Crick, decided to work on DNA even though they were meant to be doing something else. As part of their strategy to collect together evidence from different scientific disciplines, Watson went to London to hear Franklin speak about her research. He admired her results but he misunderstood her argument, and relayed a wrong version of it back to Cambridge. Armed with what they thought were Franklin's discoveries, Crick and Watson built their first model of DNA, and invited the London scientists to see it. Franklin scathingly pointed out a crucial mistake, and the head of the Cambridge laboratory ordered Crick and Watson to leave DNA alone.

But Watson was more interested in becoming

famous than in obeying the code of scientific good manners. As Franklin methodically continued her research, Watson decided to take a short cut. Behind her back, he persuaded Wilkins to show him an X-ray photograph that only Franklin, who was exceptionally skilled and systematic, had managed to obtain. The photograph showed a clear cross, the pattern obtained from a helix. It was this photograph that inspired Crick and Watson to build their famous model of the DNA double helix.

Crick and Watson happily took the credit for the discovery, which was announced in 1953. By then Franklin had left King's and moved to Birkbeck College, London, where she carried out experiments that provided precise measurements confirming and improving the original Cambridge model. Her international reputation grew, and she was invited on a lecture tour of the United States – in those days still a major expedition by ship and train.

Franklin seemed destined for a stellar career, but she was under 40 when she died of cancer. She insisted on struggling on with her work even when she was extremely ill. After her death, some scientists seemed to be eliminating her from history. Crick, Watson and Wilkins were awarded the Nobel Prize, even though it was Franklin's photograph that had provided the vital clue for the Cambridge couple.

Six years later, Watson published *The Double Helix*, a best-selling book in which he sneered at Franklin's looks, insulted her intelligence and made offensive remarks about women scientists. He later apologised, but he had probably only stated in print what many men were saying in private.

Wife of a Genius

Some historians claim that **Mileva Einstein** (1875–1948) was the true source of inspiration for Albert Einstein's revolutionary theories of physics. While they were engaged, he promised her that they would be research partners in the future. 'When you're my dear little wife,' he wrote affectionately, 'we'll diligently work on science together'.

But if he did present her ideas as his own, it does seem strange that she never published anything separately. They did discuss the new physics of relativity at home with each other, but this was probably because – like many scientists – he wanted an intelligent listener to sound out his ideas. And why did Einstein never acknowledge that she made any contributions?

Einstein may have started out with marvellous intentions, but it seems far more likely that after their marriage they slotted into a traditional relationship: he threw himself into his work, while she looked after their home and their family. Her case is sad, but also fascinating because it suggests what happened to many other female graduates – and still does.

Mileva Einstein's father seems to have been more liberal than her husband. He got special permission for her to attend an all-boys school in Zagreb (now in

Croatia), where she came top in physics and mathematics. When she went to university in Switzerland, she
found there was only one other student taking the same
courses – Albert Einstein. As they studied together, they
fell in love. His parents were furious, but after the
couple had both graduated they got married and had
two sons.

At first they were devoted to each other. Einstein said
how happy he was to have a wife who 'takes care of
everything exceptionally well, cooks well, and is always
cheerful'. Even then, right at the beginning of their
marriage, he made no mention of her ability at physics.
When they invited friends round to discuss scientific
problems, Mileva Einstein listened carefully but never
spoke.

Things soon started to go wrong. Albert Einstein's
career blossomed, but Mileva Einstein felt more and
more excluded from his life. He was becoming one of
Europe's best-known physicists, but she explained sadly
to one of her friends that 'with such fame, not much
time remains for his wife'. She became more and more
miserable and, eleven years after their marriage, she left
her husband, taking the children with her.

To get as far as university, Mileva Einstein must have
been a very clever woman. So why did she never produce any original work? One answer is that she lacked
the extra spark of determination that was essential for
women to succeed when so many obstacles were placed
in front of them. Another answer is that she married
the wrong man. Albert Einstein was so absorbed in his

own career that he did little to encourage either her independence or her cooperation. In contrast, Pierre Curie took great pains to ensure that his wife Marie had many opportunities to work and become famous in her own right.

Early Environmentalists

Intelligent and truly feminist women want two things: they want to live as women, to have masses of children by the men they love ... and they want to do their own work, whatever it may be. The two things are not compatible, except in very rare cases.

Naomi Mitchison, *Comments on Birth Control,* 1930

MOST EXPLORERS HAVE been men – but not all of them. One of the 20th century's most intrepid female travellers was Freya Stark, who wrote best-selling books about her experiences in remote parts of the world. In 1934, she revealed one secret underlying her success: 'The greatest and almost only comfort about being a woman', wrote Stark, 'is that one can always pretend to be more stupid than one is and no one is surprised'.

Stark knew that apparently harmless observers will often be allowed to see more than their supposedly more intelligent companions. Women scientists often work on what seem like unpromising areas, but they can surprise their colleagues by finding unexpected solutions to old problems. When Isaac Newton wanted to acknowledge his influential predecessors, he boasted:

'If I have seen further it is by standing on the shoulders of giants'. In contrast, during the 20th century some women were able to see further by standing at the edge of science. Feeling excluded from mainstream laboratory research, they decided to investigate the world from new angles – and they helped to shift the spotlight of scientific attention on to new topics.

Barbara McClintock was a brilliant geneticist who found it hard to get a suitable job. Although she was awarded a Nobel Prize in 1983 for her work on molecular biology and heredity, she is far less famous than Rosalind Franklin. Discoveries about human DNA have attracted massive publicity, whereas McClintock worked on corn seedlings, which seemed far less interesting. Her experiments showed that plants could change colour, suggesting the existence of 'jumping genes'. But by the 1950s, McClintock was regarded as a crank who kept putting forward theories nobody could understand. It was only twenty years later that scientists realised how significant her results were for human genetics and recognition for her achievements came extremely late in her life.

Exciting research projects attract most funding, especially if they have military or financial applications. Around the middle of the 20th century, far more money was being poured into engineering, nuclear energy and space travel than into subjects such as anthropology or oceanography. Women found it easier to get jobs in less attractive fields, where there was less money available and less competition. But scientific fashions changed towards the end of the century, and women have emerged as the pioneers in areas that once seemed relatively unimportant.

Environmental issues now hit the headlines almost every day, but as recently as 50 years ago scientists carried out experiments with little thought of the damage they might be inflicting on the world. The modern green approach was launched in 1962, when **Rachel Carson** published her path-breaking book *Silent Spring*. She accused scientists and farmers of destroying the environment by using dangerous chemicals in order to make a greater profit. This topic once seemed marginal, but now it is now central to political decision-making as well as to scientific investigations.

Other female scientists have also campaigned to make governments realise how crucial it is to protect our environment. In Africa, **Jane Goodall** and **Dian Fossey** both spent many years living close to primates, our nearest biological relatives. They stressed that it is vital to protect animals and prevent them from becoming extinct. These explorers turned their positions to their own advantage. As women, they were relegated to what seemed a backwater of research; as scientists, they showed how significant their work could be.

The Green Pioneer

One common form of gender prejudice is to say that women are closer to nature than men, and are therefore (supposedly) better at studying plants and animals. At first **Rachel Carson** (1907–64) seemed to match this stereotype – she was a superb writer who won prizes for her poetic books about the oceans and marine life. But in her mid-fifties, she wrote a very different type of book, *Silent Spring,* which accused scientists of destroying the world.

Carson loved writing, and at university in America she studied English before switching to science. After her father died she had to support her family, and she combined her twin passions – literature and marine biology – by writing information booklets for the Bureau of Fisheries. While she continued to work for the government, she also became famous for her books about the sea, which she wrote in a lyrical style as if they were poems written in prose, even though they were scientifically accurate. Carson described the environment as harmonious and beautiful, and stressed the underlying unity of nature. For example, she described how a small worm normally washed up by the tide twice a day will spontaneously follow the same pattern in an aquarium, living 'out its life in this alien place, remembering in every fibre of its small green body, the tidal rhythm of the distant sea'.

After the Second World War, people were appalled at the devastations caused by the atomic bombs dropped on Japan, and physicists were strongly criticised. Carson increased this scepticism about science by discussing the biological sciences. She had been planning a book about the origin of life, but then she realised that scientists were destroying the natural world she loved so much. Instead of writing about the beauty of nature, she decided to write a hard-hitting book exposing the dangers of chemicals. She attacked commercial companies, condemning them for sacrificing the health of the environment in order to make more profit.

Carson collected evidence from scientific experts to prove that the environment was being ruined for ever. She explained how protecting crops with insect sprays was a short-sighted policy because the lethal chemicals were killing birds and also seeping higher and higher up the food chain to harm human beings.

She lashed out at hypocrisy. Why, she asked, were so many scientists researching into insecticides? The answer, of course, was money: the chemical companies were pouring money into the universities. But this meant that it was impossible to trust reassuring statements that the chemicals were safe. She became very angry at people who complacently adopted a head-in-the-sand attitude. If they refused to accept that insecticides should be banned until absolutely solid evidence of their destructive effects had been found, then it would be too late to do anything about it.

After Carson's *Silent Spring,* the old-fashioned view that studying nature was a gentle female pastime disappeared for ever. Her book marks the beginning of a new type of environmental writing that focuses on the potentially horrific consequences of scientific progress. Issues such as global warming and genetically modified foods are no longer restricted to academic conferences, but have become urgent political problems.

A Chimpanzee Family

Jane Goodall (1934–) is famous all over the world because she has been studying chimpanzees for over 40 years. She changed people's attitudes towards animals by describing her chimpanzees as if they lived in families and experienced human emotions.

Jane Goodall was brought up on the English coast, but by the time she was eleven she had decided where she wanted to live – in Africa. And when she had saved up enough money, that was where she went. Soon after she arrived, she managed to get a job as secretary to Louis Leakey, an anthropologist who was planning to study primates. He thought that Goodall had two main qualifications for helping him: she was untrained, and so would bring a fresh eye to his projects; and she was a woman and therefore was – he believed – more in tune with animals and the primitive spirit of Africa. This attitude infuriates many modern women, but was quite common at the time.

So in 1960, Goodall and her mother went to live in the Tanzanian jungle at Gombe. The first few weeks were terrible: they both became very ill with malaria, and the chimpanzees were too frightened to let her come near them. One day Goodall noticed a male chimpanzee screaming with frustration because he could see a banana lying inside a tent. From then on, she lured the animals nearer by leaving bananas where they were easy to reach. Eventually they learned to trust her, and they treated her almost as if she were another animal – which she was! She insisted on giving each chimpanzee a name, which made it even easier to think of them as being close relatives to humans.

Within only three months she had made her first astounding discovery. Chimpanzees had always been thought of as herbivores, but she saw David Greybeard eating some meat. A few weeks later, she saw him digging for termites with a grass blade which he had carefully peeled to make it a good shape. Her discovery forced people to recognise that humans are not the only tool-making animals.

As Goodall continued with her research, she saw many ways in which chimpanzees and people behave similarly. While she was bringing up her own baby, she admired the patience of Flo, a chimpanzee mother, and tried to copy her. Goodall watched other types of human-like behaviour. After another mother died, a younger female adopted her orphaned baby; some animals chewed herbs to relieve their stomach pains. When she saw some chimpanzees dancing in front of a waterfall, Goodall claimed that they were experiencing a sense of awe resembling religious emotion.

Goodall established many conservation projects, and so helped to slow down the rate at which the chimpanzee population is shrinking. There are now several workers at Gombe who continue to study the animals and run international programmes to educate people about treating them humanely.

Goodall rapidly became a media darling who often appeared in magazines and TV shows. Many people think it is marvellous that a female scientist should become so eminent. On the other hand, perhaps her popularity is also due to traditional prejudices about women – she seems to be looking after her large community of chimpanzees as if she were the mother of an extended family.

Dying for Gorillas

At first glance **Jane Goodall** and **Dian Fossey** (1932–85) seem very similar: they were the same age, they both regarded primates as being individuals similar to people and they were both active in animal conservation. But Fossey's life was much darker, and she was murdered in a mystery which remains unsolved.

Fossey came from a wealthy American family, but money does not always make you happy, and she was very lonely as a child. After going to university she worked in a children's hospital, but then she became obsessed with gorillas. She saved up to go on a safari to Zaire, where she met Goodall's supporter Louis Leakey. She eventually persuaded him to help her set up a research centre in Rwanda. Leakey called these anthropological women his 'Ape Ladies', an insulting term which makes them sound more like circus performers than serious researchers.

Gorillas are far less friendly than chimpanzees, yet by imitating their behaviour, Fossey lived among them unharmed for 22 years. She was thrilled when one gorilla, Peanuts, reached out and touched her hand.

These gorillas were exceptionally shy because poachers had been killing them, and Fossey became determined to protect her animals as well as study their behaviour.

In order to get money for her project, Fossey left Africa for a few years to gain better academic qualifications and to generate publicity. Her book, *Gorillas in the Mist*, was very successful, but she was never able to captivate reporters in the same way as Goodall. One problem was that she refused to behave in a feminine way. If male scientists are eccentric, their habits are often seen as being endearing or a sign of genius – for example, Albert Einstein's insistence on not wearing socks (he thought it was a waste of time to mend the holes). But Fossey lost the sympathy of the media by not beautifying herself for the cameras, and by doing unconventional things like sucking sugar straight out of the packet.

Fossey also antagonised the press by emphasising violence. Instead of portraying her gorillas as loving creatures that live together like human families, she wrote gruesome descriptions of their brutal behaviour. She also provided grisly details of gorilla corpses mutilated by hunters who sold their heads for wall decorations and their hands and feet as ashtrays. To stop this cruel gorilla trade, Fossey organised a small group of guards who trapped and punished local thieves. When she herself was murdered in her mountain cabin, it seemed clear that this was a revenge killing, but the culprit has never been caught.

FUTURE

Future

If you're a woman, you'll be called strident if you stand up for yourself, whereas a man who does the same is seen as tough and principled. I don't stay awake at night fretting about it.

Susan Greenfield, on *Tomorrow's People*, 2003

THE MOST HOPEFUL message for the future is that the status of women in science recently has been rapidly improving. It now seems unbelievable that as recently as the 1980s, many Oxford and Cambridge colleges still only took men, or that in the 1950s, women were banned from entering the Princeton physics building in case they distracted the researchers.

Throughout the world, almost all universities are now open to women as well as to men. In many countries campaigners no longer struggle for equal gender access, because that battle has already been won. Instead, they are fighting to make sure that children from poorer homes, often from minority ethnic groups, have the same opportunities as those with wealthy parents.

Scientific societies are trying hard to increase the proportion of their women members. At London's Royal Society, over 10 per cent of the new Fellows elected each year are now women. Female scientists agree that women should not be promoted too rapidly, because they oppose positive discrimination (affirmative action) – they want to be confident that they have been chosen for their scientific excellence, not simply for being a woman. They argue that favouritism would breed prejudice, not eliminate it.

Eminent female scientists are enthusiastic about encouraging girls to take up science. Some of them wear glamorous clothes because they want to dispel the myth that women who do science are frumpish freaks. If you look around any modern university, hospital or laboratory, you will see plenty of well-dressed, attractive women who hold top positions.

But, but, but … all the statistics show that there are still far fewer women than men in senior posts. Why is this? Does it mean that women are still being discriminated against? Or could it perhaps be that some men are right – women are intrinsically less good at science? Before rushing to conclusions, it's important to examine the reasons for the differences between men and women working in science.

One reassuring explanation is that it takes time for the effects of better education to filter through. Thirty-plus years into the future, girls leaving school today will be at the peak of their professional careers, and there will be a far higher proportion of women in the best jobs. There will be more women in scientific societies, more women running laboratories, more women heading universities and educational organisations.

Another reason why fewer girls go into science at present is that not everyone wants to be a pioneer. It is still unfortunately true that young women in a physics or engineering class at university may find themselves alone, surrounded by male students and male teachers. This can be intimidating, and some girls sensibly decide to opt for a subject where they will feel more at ease. Again, this will change when a snowball effect starts coming into operation: as more female students go for the traditionally male subjects, so it will become easier for others to join them. When more women qualify and get promoted to senior levels, they will become role models for students to emulate.

Governments are intervening to make it easier for mothers to be professional scientists. Women no longer need feel that they have to make an agonising choice between having babies or building a career. Some organisations now offer both parents periods of leave when they have a baby, and they also provide child-care arrangements. Even if mothers do decide to devote several years to looking after their family, it is becoming far more realistic for them to assume that they can get back on the job ladder and be promoted.

Women who have already managed to get high-up posts in science are starting programmes to help younger women succeed. As well as giving talks to undergraduates, they are setting up advice networks, and establishing mentoring schemes in which two women of different ages exchange information and opinions. Some enlightened university departments are asking women's groups for help to make their working environment more female-friendly.

Nevertheless, many women argue that discrimination does still exist in science. They maintain that because it has been made illegal, it has become more difficult to detect. Laboratory leaders may give their male students more interesting research topics, or discuss new ideas with their colleagues in sports clubs and other places where women are less likely to go. Babies are treated differently from the moment they are born. Boys are often encouraged to be more outspoken and daring than girls, and these characteristics may give them an advantage in interviews. Sometimes men don't even realise that they're being unfair – although they think that they are treating both sexes equally, subconsciously they believe that science should be a male world.

Disappointingly, signs of success can be misleading. I spoke to a female researcher at Cambridge University, who explained: 'I've won a 3-year contract to carry out my own project, and to outsiders, this seems extremely impressive. However, more women than men apply for this sort of funding, because officially, I'm working in someone else's laboratory. And as I'm not teaching, it'll be difficult for me to get a lecturing position later on. Men are very reluctant to take these positions because they want to feel independent and are anxious to get promoted as soon as possible. After three years, I'll no longer have a job.'

Conversely, women still in lower positions are not

necessarily being discriminated against. One exciting modern development is that women are making their own decisions about what sort of life they want to lead. I met a senior scientist in London who has turned down several offers of promotion, and so has not been appointed the director of her laboratory. 'What's the use of earning more money', she protested, 'if I'm too busy to enjoy it, and if I'm doing office work instead of the science that I love?'

Women are making their own choices – and they are often different from men's. Instead of striving for the best-paid jobs, they are examining which aspects of their work give them most pleasure. Do they prefer scientific research or high-level administration? Do they want to be committed to their laboratory or university seven days a week, or would they rather spend time doing other activities?

Some women have decided that ambition and cut-throat competition are for men: they prefer to earn less money, but to lead richer lives. The women in this book were not afraid to think and behave differently from other people. Not all of them were famous, but by changing themselves they helped to change the world. And that's what you can do too.

Further Reading

Alic, Margaret. *Hypatia's heritage: a history of women in science from antiquity to the late nineteenth century* (London: The Women's Press, 1986).

Dry, Sarah. *Curie* (London: Haus, 2003).

Fara, Patricia. *Pandora's breeches: women, science and power* (London: Pimlico, 2004).

Gates, Barbara and Shteir, Ann (eds). *Natural eloquence: women reinscribe science* (Wisconsin: University of Wisconsin Press, 1989).

Haines, Catharine M.C. *International women in science: a biographical dictionary to 1950* (Santa Barbara and Oxford: ABC-Clio, 2001).

Ogilvie, Marilyn Bailey. *Women in science: antiquity through the nineteenth century: a biographical dictionary with annotated bibliography* (Cambridge, MA: MIT Press, 1996).

Ogilvie, Marilyn and Harvey, Joy (eds). *Biographical dictionary of women in science* (London: Routledge, 2000).

Schiebinger, Londa. *The mind has no sex? Women in the origins of modern science* (Cambridge and London: Harvard University Press, 1989).

Illustrations

Figure 1. Minerva directing study to the attainment of Universal Knowledge. Frontispiece of *The New Encyclopædia*, 1807. By permission of the British Library, shelfmark 012217.c.1

Figure 2. Nobel Prize medal for chemistry and physics. Website: http://www.nobel.se/nobel/medals/physics-chemistry.html

Figure 3. Margaret Cavendish (Duchess of Newcastle) and her family. Frontispiece of Margaret Cavendish, *Natures Pictures Drawn by Fancies Pencil to the Life* (London, for J. Martin and J. Allestyre, 1656). Original by Abraham van Diepenbeke, engraved by Peter Clouwet. By permission of the Syndics of Cambridge University Library

Figure 4. Elisabetha and Johannes Hevelius observing with their great sextant. Johannes Hevelius, *Machina cœlestis* (Danzig, 1673), facing p. 222. By permission of the Syndics of Cambridge University Library

Figure 5. Louise Bourgeois. Frontispiece of Louise Bourgeois, *Observations diverses sur la sterilité, perte de fruit, foecondité, accouchements et maladies des femmes et enfants nouveaux naiz*, 1609. Wellcome Library, London

Figure 6. Euphrosyne learns about electricity. Benjamin Martin, *The young gentlemen's and ladies philosophy* (2 vols, London, 1759–63), vol. 1, facing p. 301. By permission of the Syndics of Cambridge University Library

Figure 7. Mrs Bryan with two girls. Frontispiece of Margaret Bryan, *A compendious system of astronomy* (1797). Engraving by

W. Nutter from a 1797 miniature by Samuel Shelley. By permission of the Syndics of Cambridge University Library

Figure 8. *Caroline and William Herschel.* Coloured lithograph after Alfred Diethe, c. 1896. Wellcome Library, London

Figure 9. Marie Paulze and her husband Antoine Lavoisier. Jacques-Louis David, 1788. The Metropolitan Museum of Art, Purchase, Mr and Mrs Charles Wrightsman Gift, in honour of Everett Fahy, 1977 (1977.10)

Figure 10. Marie Paulze Lavoisier: her sketch of the laboratory. Marie Paulze Lavoisier, 'Experiments on the respiration of a man carrying out work', probably 1790–91. Reproduced from Grimaux, *Lavoisier*

Figure 11. Clémence Royer. *Les Hommes d'Aujourd'Hui,* vol. 4, number 170, 1881.

Figure 12. Mary Anning. Painting by William Gray, 1942.

Figure 13. A photograph of Miranda Stuart/James Barry in Jamaica, around 1860. Wellcome Library, London

Figure 14. Teaching staff at Cambridge in 1896. Reproduced by courtesy of the Principal and Fellows of Newnham College, Cambridge.

Figure 15. Grace Hopper in naval uniform. Photographed by James S. Davis. Official U.S. Navy photography from the collections of the Naval Historical Centre

Figure 16 Marie Curie. Caricature of Pierre and Marie Curie by Julius Mendes Price, *Vanity Fair,* 1904.

Figure 17. Dorothy Hodgkin. Maggi Hambling, 1985, oil on canvas. National Portrait Gallery, London, NPG 5797

INDEX OF NAMES

Collections of classic poetry and prose
Edited by Kate Agnew

Wizard's collections of classic poetry and prose, introduced by some of the best-loved authors for young people, are a rollercoaster ride of emotions and experience, expressed in some of the most passionate words ever written.

'Books to curl up with ... these are substantial anthologies and the choice is rich indeed. Endlessly refreshing and intriguing ... there's never a dull moment.' *Guardian*

'Wonderful ... dispels preconceptions and encourages new audiences' *Booktrusted*

'At a time when jaunty modern verse proliferates, it's good to have such well-chosen collections of poems on the most exciting subject areas of all.' Adèle Geras, *Armadillo*

'The selection and arrangement of material is brilliant, creating cross-currents, complications, and time travelling coincidences.' *Times Educational Supplement*

All royalties from these books will go to the charity National Children's Homes   the children's charity

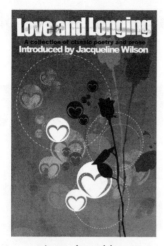

Introduced by
Jacqueline Wilson
ISBN 1 84046 523 9

Introduced by
Kevin Crossley-Holland
ISBN 1 84046 526 3

Introduced by
Philip Pullman
ISBN 1 84046 567 0

Introduced by
Michael Morpurgo
ISBN 1 84046 570 0

UK £5.99 • Canada $12.00

Darkness Visible: Inside the World of Philip Pullman

Nicholas Tucker

Philip Pullman is one of the world's most popular and original authors, read by children and adults alike. Containing an astonishing cast of characters, from scholarly Oxford dons to armoured bears, witches, angels, murderous Spectres and hideous harpies drawn straight from Greek mythology, Pullman's fiction can be read at many different levels.

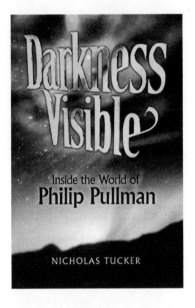

Darkness Visible looks at the world of Philip Pullman, from the flamboyant *Sally Lockhart* series and the award winning *Clockwork* and *I Was a Rat!*, to the epic *His Dark Materials* trilogy. It shows the diverse influences – from Milton and Blake to comic books and radio drama – that have shaped his writing and uncovers the part played by Pullman's unconventional childhood.

Written by acclaimed critic Nicholas Tucker, and packed with never-before-seen family photos, illustrations from Pullman's beloved graphic novels and fresh material from recent interviews, this is both a celebration of Philip Pullman and a useful guide to the rich world of his fiction.

UK £6.99 • Canada $15.00 • ISBN 1 84046 482 8

Dear Mr Morpingo: Inside the World of Michael Morpurgo

Geoff Fox

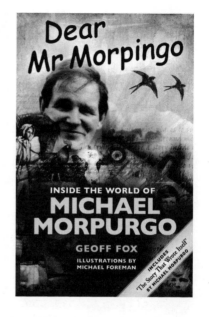

Dr Mr Morpingo

*I have just read your book
The Wreck of the Zanzibar.
It's the best book I have ever
read. It is miles better than
any Harry Potter book. BUT,
there's one thing definitely wrong
with this book. It's about a girl.
Write me a book about a boy
who gets stuck on a desert
island.*

Michael Morpurgo may be
the Children's Laureate, but
readers often have trouble
spelling his name correctly. Yet thousands and thousands of
them have no trouble at all reading stories like *The Butterfly Lion,
Cool!* or *Private Peaceful*. Or *Kensuke's Kingdom*, the best-selling
story Michael wrote about a boy stranded on a desert island to
please his fan.

Dear Mr Morpingo takes you inside the world of Michael
Morpurgo to answer the questions readers love to ask – about
Michael's life, the ideas behind his stories and how he writes.

UK £5.99 • Canada $12.00 • ISBN 1 84046 607 3

Big Numbers: A mind-expanding trip to infinity and back

Mary and John Gribbin
Illustrated by
*Ralph Edney and
Nicholas Halliday*

How big is infinity? How small is an electron?

When will the Sun destroy the Earth?

How fast is a nerve impulse in your brain?

Why can't you see inside a black hole?

What's the hottest temperature ever recorded on Earth?

What's the furthest you can see on a clear night?

Welcome to the amazing world of 'Big Numbers', where you'll travel from the furthest reaches of the known Universe to the tiniest particles that make up life on Earth. Together with Mary and John Gribbin, you can find out how our telescopes can see 10 billion years into the past, and why a thimbleful of a neutron star would contain as much mass as all the people on Earth put together!

UK £6.99 • Canada $15.00 • ISBN 1 84046 661 8